Contents

About the Chef

Hello, I am Chef Sharon, daughter of the late Mr. George E. and Mrs. Jennie V. Watts. Born in Gainesville, Florida, though, raised and nurtured in a subdivision called Copeland, which is located on the outskirts of Gainesville. At the present 'Copeland' is my home. I have nine siblings, six wonderful in-laws, and an abundance of nieces and nephews. Also, I am fortunate to be the godparent of seven godchildren. Copeland's population includes many relatives and close friends of mine. This place shares great memories of playing outside with my siblings, cousins, and neighbors until dusk.

The name "Copeland's Culinary Eats" was established from the good home cooking I enjoyed as a child. Mom would call my siblings and I in the house when it was time to eat dinner. My parents taught me how to cook, which help catapult me even further into my endeavors. So, it is no surprise cooking and baking are my hobbies. On a more personal note, I have experience in Human Resources, management, and training. Author of two books and a licensed minister.

In 2019, I took my knowledge to the next level by attending and graduating from Auguste Escoffier School of Culinary Arts in June of 2020. In addition, I obtained my SERV Safe Certification as a Certified Food Manager. My plans in early 2021 includes a continuation of my Facebook Live cooking show. In the Fall of 2021, I endeavor to own and operating a mobile 2021 food truck.

This cookbook is formatted different than the typical cookbook. In most cookbooks, you will see the measurement before the item. Example: ½ Cup of Sugar. Nevertheless, in this cookbook, the item is first, then the measurement. Example: Sugar – ½ Cups. Why? I am self-diagnosed with dyslexia. I see letters, phrase, and words in reverse. Due to that fact, it became difficult to learn as a child. I became aware of this 'eureka moment' in my early twenties. So, I took it upon myself to truly focus when reading. Hear the conclusion of the matter; it is easier for me to understand a recipe better by listing the item first, then the measurement. With that being said, I hope you enjoy these recipes. Looking forward to sharing with you in the spring of 2021...

Final words of encouragement to aspiring chefs; stay focus and on course during your journey regardless of the many obstacles. Do not be afraid to create out of the box and always ask questions for clarification. When life gets busy, take a breath, rest, and get back in the game. Allow the words of Apostle Paul to guide you; "For I can do everything through Christ, who gives me strength." Philippians 4:13

Let us get cooking!
Chef Sharon

My favourite herbs and spices!

Spices

Cooking and Baking Tips

Dices and Slices Examples

Minimum Internal Cooking Temperatures

• Ground Chuck or Beef	160ºF
• Ground Chicken or Turkey	165ºF
• Beef Steaks	145ºF
• Chicken	165ºF
• Fish	145ºF
• Leftovers and casseroles	165ºF

- Shrimp, lobster, crab, and scallops cook until flesh is white
- Clams, oysters, and mussels until shell opens while cooking

How to Properly Store Food in the Refrigerator

Top to Bottom

1) Ready to eat foods
2) Raw Fish
3) Raw Steak
4) Raw Pork
5) Raw Ground Meats
6) Raw Chicken

Basic Measurement Steps

	1 Gallon	Quart	Pint	Cup	Oz
1 Gallon		4 Quarts	8 Pints	16 Cups	128 Ounces
1 Quart			2 Pints	4 Cups	32 Ounces
1 Pint				2 Cups	16 Ounces
1 Cup					8 Ounces

Tablespoons and Teaspoons

1/2	Tablespoon	=	1 1/2	Teaspoon
1	Tablespoon	=	3	Teaspoon
2	Tablespoon	=	6	Teaspoon
3	Tablespoon	=	9	Teaspoon
4	Tablespoon	=	1/4	Cup
8	Tablespoon	=	1/2	Cup
12	Tablespoon	=	3/4	Cup
16	Tablespoon	=	1	Cup

Fractions of an inch

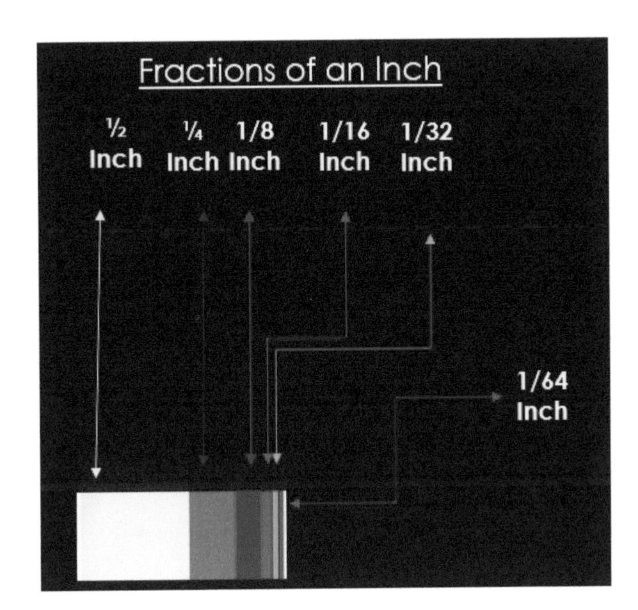

Cooking Terminology

1) Al dente — Especially of pasta, cooked so as not to be too soft, firm to the bite.
2) Baste — to moisten (meat or other food) while cooking, with drippings, butter, etc.
3) Blanch — to scald briefly and then drain, as peaches.
4) Brine — water saturated or strongly impregnated with salt.
5) Broil — to cook by direct heat, as on a gridiron over the heat or in an oven under the heat.
6) Carryover Cooking —when you cook a food and remove it from the heat, it will continue to cook internally as the heat leaves the food.
7) Chiffonade — a mixture of finely cut vegetables, herbs, or the like, for use in soups, salads, etc.
8) Coarsely chop — to chop something into relatively uneven pieces, without much attention to size and shape.
9) Cream - soften a fat, such as butter, by beating it until light and fluffy. Butter and sugar are often creamed together to make an aerated paste.
10) Cut in — To work a solid fat into dry ingredients, such as butter and flour when making pie crust. This is usually done with a pastry blender, cutter, or your fingertips. You can also use a food processor.
11) Deglaze — to add wine or other liquid to a pan in which meat has been roasted or sauteed to make a sauce that incorporates the cooking juices.
12) Degrease —to remove grease from. To remove fat from the surface of food. This is most done by skimming fat off the top of stews, soups, or stock while they cook. This can also be done by placing the liquid in the refrigerator and allowing the fat to form a solid layer on top, which can then be easily removed.
13) Dice — to cut into small cubes.
14) Dredge — to sprinkle or coat with some powdered substance, especially flour. Dredging adds flavor and texture to fried foods, as the coating crisps up and takes on a darker color.

15) Fold – To gently combine wet and dry ingredients in a folding motion, using a large, flat spatula.
16) Fry - to cook in a pan or on a griddle over direct heat, usually in fat or oil.
17) Grill - to broil a steak. to scorch, make extremely hot.
18) Julienne – of food, especially vegetables cut into thin strips or small, matchlike pieces.
19) Leavening – a substance used to produce fermentation in dough or batter.
20) Lukewarm – moderately warm; lukewarm:
21) Marinate- to steep food in **a** marinade.
22) Mince – to cut or chop into exceedingly small pieces.
23) Mix - to combine into one mass, collection, or assemblage, generally with a thorough blending of the constituents.
24) Parboil - to boil partially or for a short time; precook.
25) Pare - to cut off the outer coating, layer, or part of.
26) Peel - to strip something of its skin, rind, bark, etc.: to peel an orange.
27) Pinch – a small amount of any dry ingredient.
28) Poach – to cook eggs, fish, fruits, etc. in a hot liquid that is kept just below the boiling point.
29) Puree – a cooked food, especially a vegetable or fruit, that has been put through a sieve, blender, or the like.
30) Reduce – to decrease the volume of a liquid by simmering it, which causes evaporation. This makes the liquid thicker and intensifies its flavor. The resulting thicker liquid is called a "reduction."
31) Render - to try out oil from fat, blubber, etc., by melting.
32) Rest – To remove a food from the heat, then let it sit for a set period before cutting.
33) Roast - to bake meat or other food uncovered, especially in an oven.
34) Roux - a cooked mixture of butter or other fat and flour used to thicken sauces, soups, etc.
35) Sachet – a small bag made of cheesecloth, stuffed with whole spices and herbs. Sachets are usually tied with cooking twice and left to simmer in broths, stocks, sauces, and other cooking liquids to infuse them with the flavor of the herbs.
36) Scald – to heat to a temperature just short of the boiling point:
37) Score – to cut shallow slices on the surface of a food.
38) Sear – to burn or char the surface of: She seared the steak to seal in the juices.
39) Section – to cut or divide into sections. to cut through to present a section.

40) Shred - to cut or tear into small pieces, especially small strips; reduce to shreds:
41) Shuck — to remove or discard as or like shucks; peel off:
42) Sieve — an instrument with a meshed or perforated bottom, used for separating coarse from fine parts of loose matter, for straining liquids, etc., especially one with a circular frame and fine meshes or perforations.
43) Simmer - to cook or cook in a liquid at or just below the boiling point.
44) Skim — to take up or remove (floating matter) from the surface of a liquid, as with a spoon or ladle.
45) Sliver - any small, narrow piece or portion.
46) Steam - to expose to or treat with steam, as to heat, cook, soften, renovate, or the like.
47) Stew - to undergo cooking by simmering or slow boiling.
48) Steep - to soak in water or other liquid, as to soften, cleanse, or extract some constituent:
49) Stir - to move one's hand or an implement continuously or repeatedly through (a liquid or other substance) to cool, mix, agitate, dissolve, etc., any or all the component parts:
50) Stir Fry - to cook (food) quickly by cutting into small pieces and stirring constantly in a lightly oiled wok or frying pan over high heat: a common method of Chinese cookery.
51) Sweat (as in, sweat the onions) — Cooking vegetables slowly, over low heat, in a small amount of fat. The pan is usually covered to prevent steam from escaping.
52) Toast - to brown, as bread or cheese, by exposure to heat.
53) Truss — to tie, bind, or fasten. To make fast with skewers, thread, or the like, as the wings or legs of a fowl in preparation for cooking.
54) Whip - an act of whisking. a rapid, sweeping stroke; light, rapid movement.
55) Zest - The fragrant, outermost layer of citrus rind. The zest is the paper-thin layer that colors the skin. To zest means to gently remove this outer layer from a citrus fruit with a paring knife or fine-tooth grater (called a "zester"). A fraction of a millimeter beneath the zest is the white pith, which is bitter and unwanted; so, when zesting, you do not want to grate so hard that you reveal the white pith.

Appetizers

Alaskan Crab Bisque

Total Minutes: 1 Hour 40 Minutes
Prep Time: 20 Minutes
Cook Time: 80 Minutes
Servings: 6 to 8

Ingredients

- Alaskan Crab Meat from 5 Clusters
- Alaskan Crab Shells from 5 Clusters
- Bay Leaves - 2
- Water – 10 Cups
- Butter - 4 Tablespoons Butter
- All-Purpose Flour - 4 Tablespoons
- Heavy Cream – ½ Cup
- Onion – 1 Medium Sized, Pureed
- Celery- 2 Stalks, Pureed
- Minced Garlic – 1 Teaspoon
- Old Bay Seasoning – ½ Teaspoon
- White Wine – 1 Cup
- Salt
- Pepper
- Parsley Flakes

Let us get to cooking!

1) Remove the crab meat from the clusters, set aside.
2) Place the crab shells and bay leaves in a 6-quart stockpot. Add 10 cups of water to cover the shells. Cook on medium to high heat for an hour.
3) Drain the crab stock by placing a piece of large cheesecloth over a large bowl to catch the crab shells. Throw out the crab shells. Set aside the crab stock.
4) In the same 6-quart stockpot, melt butter over low heat. Add the flour, cook until golden brown.
5) Add the heavy cream, onions, celery, minced garlic, and old bay Seasoning. Stir to combine. Add the white wine, parsley flakes and salt and pepper to taste.
6) Pour in 4 cups of the crab stock.
7) Turn the temperature to medium heat and continue stirring until the mixture thickens. Let simmer for 10 minutes. Enjoy.

Brandy Shrimp Scampi

Total Minutes: 30 Minutes
Prep Time: 15 Minutes

Cook Time: 15 Minutes
Servings: 4 to 6

Ingredients

- Uncooked Shrimp, Deveined - 1 Lb. Medium Sized
- Spaghetti Pasta – 1 Box, Follow Cooking Instructions
- Butter – 1 Stick
- Olive Oil - 8 Tablespoons
- Minced Garlic - 2 Tablespoons
- Parsley Flakes, Dried - 2 Tablespoons or Fresh – 3 Tablespoons Chopped
- Lemon Pepper - 2 Teaspoons
- Brandy - 1 Cup

Let us get to cooking!

1) In a 3-quart sauté pan, melt butter, add olive oil and minced garlic, cook until garlic is aromatic.
2) Add the shrimp, 2 tablespoons of fresh or 1 tablespoon of dried parsley and lemon pepper cook and stir until shrimp turns pink.
3) Add Brandy. Let simmer one-two minutes. Add cooked pasta just to coat. Enjoy!

Like a Greek Salad

Total Minutes: 20 Minutes
Prep Time: 20 Minutes
Cook Time: 0 Minutes
Servings: 5

Ingredients

- Cherry Tomatoes – 1 small container, sliced or whole
- Black Olives – ½ cup, sliced
- Green Olives – ½ cup, sliced
- Bell Pepper – 1 small dice
- Red Onions – ½ Onion, thinly sliced
- Cucumbers – 2 medium sized chopped (Skin on or off)
- Feta cheese – ½ Cup
- Rosemary – 1 teaspoon, chopped
- Olive Oil, 1/3 Cup
- Lime Juice – 3 teaspoons
- Salt to taste

Let us get to cooking!

1) Combine all ingredients into a large bowl, toss until combined. Enjoy!

Onion Rings

Total Minutes: 30 Minutes
Prep Time: 15 Minutes
Cook Time: 15 Minutes
Servings: 2

Ingredients

- Onions – 1 Large Sized, Sliced ¼ Inch
- Self-Rising White Corn Meal – 1 Cup
- Lemon Pepper, 2 Tablespoons
- Cayenne Pepper, ¼ Teaspoon
- Salt – ¼ Teaspoon
- Eggs – 3, Beaten
- Beer – 3 Tablespoons
- Vegetable Oil

Let us get to cooking!

- Pull apart onion rings and place in the freezer while prepping ingredients.
- Line a cookie sheet with paper towels to drain the excess oil off the onion rings.
- In a medium sized bowl mix the self-rising white corn meal, lemon pepper, cayenne pepper and salt.
- In another medium sized bowl beat the eggs and beer.
- Heat vegetable oil to 350ºF in a 3-quart sauté pan.
- Dip the onion rings a few at a time into the eggs, then coat with the corn meal mixture. Repeat.
- Place battered onion ring in oil, fry until golden brown.
- Place the fried onion rings onto the paper towel to drain.
- Enjoy with my Homemade Ranch Dressing or a dressing of your choice

Fried Green Tomatoes

Total Minutes: **30 Minutes**
Prep Time: **15 Minutes**
Cook Time: **15 Minutes**
Servings: **4 - 5**

Ingredients

- Green Tomato – 1 Large Sized, Slice like an apple
- Self-Rising White Corn Meal – 1 Cup
- Lemon Pepper, 2 Teaspoons
- Salt – ½ Teaspoon
- Eggs – 2
- Water – 3 Tablespoons
- Vegetable Oil

Let us get to cooking!

1) Line a cookie sheet with paper towels to drain the excess oil off the tomato's rings.
2) Mix the self-rising white corn meal, lemon pepper and salt. Set aside.
3) Beat eggs and water in medium sized bowl.
4) Heat vegetable oil to 350ºF in a -quart sauté pan.
5) Dip tomatoes in the egg wash, then coat with the self-rising corn meal, repeat.
6) Fry until golden brown. Place the fried tomatoes onto the paper towel to drain.
7) Enjoy with my Homemade Ranch Dressing or a dressing of your choice.

Chicken Noodle Soup

Total Minutes: 1 Hour 30 Minutes
Prep Time: 30 Minutes
Cook Time: 1 Hour
Servings: 6 to 8

Ingredients

- Olive Oil – 4 Tablespoons
- Yellow Onions – 2 Small or Medium Sized Onions
- 2 Bell Peppers – Medium Sized (Variety of Colors, Optional)
- Celery – 1 Cup Chopped into Small Pieces
- Butter – 4 Tablespoons
- Flour – 3 Tablespoons
- Chicken Breast – 1 Lb.
- Lemon Pepper – 2 Tablespoons
- Poultry Seasoning – 2 Tablespoons
- Parsley Flakes, Dried or Fresh – 1 Tablespoon
- Chicken Bouillon – 5 Small
- Carrots – 1 Small Bag Shredded
- Water – 12 Cups
- Salt to Taste
- Egg Noodles – 1 12oz Bag

Let us get to cooking!

1) In a 6-quart stockpot, heat the olive oil under medium to high heat.
2) Add the onions, bell Peppers and celery, cook until tender.
3) Add the butter, let it melt.
4) Add the flour, cook until the flour is Golden Brown.
5) Add the seasonings, lemon pepper, poultry seasoning, chicken bouillon, stir until combined.
6) Add the water, chicken, and carrots. Stir to combine. Cook for 1 hour.
7) Salt to taste. Add the Egg Noodles, cook for 5 minutes. Enjoy.

Chicken Salad

Total Minutes: 30 Minutes
Prep Time: 30 Minutes
Cook Time: 0 Minutes
Servings: 5

Ingredients

- Cooked Chicken Breast – 1 Lb., Pulled or Diced
- Pureed Onions – ½ Cup
- Pureed Celery – ½ Cup
- Dried Thyme – 2 Teaspoons
- Lemon Pepper – 2 Teaspoons
- Celery Salt – ½ Teaspoon
- Red Bell Pepper – 1 Small Dice
- Grapes – 1 Cups, Sliced
- Mayonnaise – ¾ Cup
- Mustard – ¼ Cup

Let us get to cooking!

1) Combine all ingredients into a large bowl, mix until combined.
2) Enjoy with crackers, chips or as a sandwich.

Ranch Salad Wedge

Total Minutes: **30 Minutes**
Prep Time: **20 Minutes**
Cook Time: **10 Minutes**
Servings: **4**

Ingredients

- Iceberg Lettuce – 1 head, quartered
- Cucumber – 1 Small Dice, skin on or off
- Tomato – 1 Small Dice
- Carrots – ½ Cup shredded
- Cooked Bacon – 3 slices, crumbled
- Homemade Ranch Dressing
- Cheddar Cheese – ½ cup shredded

Let us get to cooking!

1) Assemble the salad by pouring the homemade ranch dressing (see recipe) on top of the salad wedge, then sprinkle other ingredients on top or around the salad wedge. Enjoy.

Spinach Chickpea Hummus

Total Minutes: 15 Minutes
Prep Time: 15 Minutes
Cook Time: 0 Minutes
Servings: 5

Ingredients

- Handful of Fresh Spinach
- Chickpeas – 1 Can 15oz
- Lemon Juice – 4 Tablespoons
- Tahini – 3 Tablespoons
- Garlic Clove – 2 Cloves
- Olive Oil – 2 Tablespoons
- Red or Cayenne Pepper – ½ Teaspoon
- Salt to Taste

Let us get to cooking!

1) Drain the water off the chickpeas. Set aside.
2) In a blender or food processor, blend the spinach, chickpeas, lemon juice, tahini, garlic, olive oil, red/cayenne pepper, and salt until thoroughly mixed and smooth.
3) Add liquid from soybeans until desired consistency, creamy and paste-like.
4) Remove the hummus from the blender into a bowl with a lid, refrigerate for 1 hour.
5) Enjoy with your favorite crackers or chips.

Chicken Salad Rolls

Total Minutes: 4 Hours
Prep Time: 3 Hours 30 Minutes
Cook Time: 30 Minutes
Servings: 20

Ingredients

- Mashed Sweet Potatoes – ½ Cup
- Reserved Sweet Potato Water – ½ Cup (Water from the cooked potatoes)
- Butter – ½ Cup
- Sugar – ½ Cup
- Salt – 1 Teaspoon
- Hot Water – ½ Cup
- Fleischmann Instant Dry Yeast, 1 pack
- Eggs – 1
- All Purpose Flour – 4 Cups

Let us get to cooking!

1) Combine mashed sweet potatoes, reserved sweet potato water, butter, sugar, salt, hot water, set aside.
2) Combine Fleischmann's Instant Dry Yeast and all-purpose flour, mix, set aside.
3) Add Eggs to potato mixture, stir, then add flour mixture- two cups at a time.
4) Knead 5 to 7 minutes
5) Place in a bowl greased with olive oil, coat the dough, then cover to rise about 1 hour in a warm spot. The dough should double in size.
6) Punch the dough with your fist, cut dough in half. Set aside.

Chicken Salad Rolls Continued:

Chicken Salad
Ingredients

- Cooked Chicken Breast – 1 Lb., Pulled
- Pureed Onions – 1 Cup
- Pureed Celery – ½ Cup
- Dried Thyme – 2 Teaspoons
- Lemon Pepper – 2 Teaspoons
- Celery Salt – ¼ Teaspoon
- Red Bell Pepper – 1 Small Dice
- Mozzarella Cheese – 2 Cups

Let us get to cooking!

1) Combine all Ingredients (except for the cheese) into a large bowl, toss until combined.

Time to assemble.

1) Pre-heat oven to 350F.
2) Roll dough onto a surface, lightly coated with flour. Roll into a rectangle. Spread the chicken salad mixture on the dough evenly. Lengthwise, roll the dough. Cut into 10 slices. Place on greased cookie sheet or baking pan. Let the dough rise 30 minutes or until doubled in size.
3) Sprinkle Mozzarella Cheese over the top. Bake for 20-25 minutes. Enjoy!

Salad Dressings

Spreads

Homemade Ranch Salad Dressing

Total Minutes: 10 Minutes
Prep Time: 10 Minutes
Cook Time: 0 Minutes
Servings: 10

Ingredients

- Mayonnaise - 1 Cup
- Sour Cream - 1 Cup
- Buttermilk - 1/3 Cup (Add More for A Looser Dressing)
- Chives - 1 Teaspoon
- Garlic Powder - 1 Teaspoon
- Onion Powder - 1 Teaspoon
- Black Pepper - 1 Teaspoon
- Red Pepper - 1/2 Teaspoon
- Salt to Taste

Let us get to cooking!

1) Add all ingredients in a bowl or blender and mix/blend well.
2) Enjoy with your salads, hot wings, onion rings, etc.

Black Berry Vinaigrette

Total Minutes: 10 Minutes
Prep Time: 10 Minutes
Cook Time: 0 Minutes
Servings: 8

Ingredients

- Blackberries – ½ Cup
- Garlic Powder - ¼ Teaspoon
- Onion Powder - ¼ Teaspoon
- Black Pepper - ¼ Teaspoon
- Basil - ¼ Teaspoon
- Parsley - ¼ Teaspoon
- Oregano - ¼ Teaspoon
- Thyme - ¼ Teaspoon
- Salt - ¼ Teaspoon
- Balsamic Vinegar – 1 Cup
- Olive Oil – ½ Cup

Let us get to cooking!

1) Add ingredients in a bowl or blender and mix/blend well.
2) Enjoy with your salads, hot wings, onion rings, etc.

Italian Dressing

Total Minutes: 10 Minutes
Prep Time: 10 Minutes
Cook Time: 0 Minutes
Servings: 8

Ingredients

- Garlic Powder – ¼ Teaspoon
- Onion Powder – ¼ Teaspoon
- Freshly Ground Pepper – ¼ Teaspoon
- Basil – ¼ Teaspoon
- Parsley – ¼ Teaspoon
- Oregano – ¼ Teaspoon
- Thyme – ½ Teaspoon
- Celery Salt – ¼ Teaspoon
- Salt – ½ Teaspoon
- Apple Cider Vinegar – ¼ Cup
- Olive Oil – 2/3 Cup
- Water – 3 Tablespoons

Let us get mixing.

1) Add ingredients in a bowl or blender and mix/blend well.
2) Enjoy with your salads, hot wings, onion rings, etc.

Rosemary Garlic Whipped Butter

Total Minutes: 10 Minutes
Prep Time: 10 Minutes
Cook Time: 0 Minutes
Servings: 8

Ingredients

- Heavy Cream – 1 Cup
- Garlic Powder – ¼ Teaspoon
- Crushed Rosemary – 2 Teaspoons
- Salt – Pinch

Let us get mixing.

1) Add all ingredients in a hand blender.
   Blend until the heavy cream is thickened. About 2 Minutes.
2) Refrigerate. Enjoy on toast, bagels etc.

Lemon Pepper Butter

Total Minutes:	**10 Minutes**
Prep Time:	**10 Minutes**
Cook Time:	**0 Minutes**
Servings:	**8**

Ingredients

1) Organic Heavy Cream with a High Fat Content – 1 Cup
2) Lemon Pepper – 1 Teaspoons
3) Salt – Pinch

Let us get mixing.

1) Add the heavy cream in a hand blender. Blend until the heavy cream separates into buttermilk and butter. Blend about 2-3 minutes.
2) Place Cheesecloth over a bowl to drain the buttermilk. Squeeze the butter that remains in the cheesecloth to release the residual buttermilk.
3) Place the butter in another bowl, add the lemon pepper fold in until the pepper is well blended into the butter.
4) Refrigerate. Enjoy on veggies or meats.

Entrees

Season 17 Baked Chicken

Total Minutes: 1 Hour 20 Minutes
Prep Time: 20 Minutes
Cook Time: 1 Hour
Servings: 6 to 8

Ingredients

- Chicken – 1 Whole or cut into 8 pieces
- Onions – 1
- Season 17 as needed – 2 Tablespoons
- Lemon Pepper – 2 Tablespoons
- Crushed Rosemary – 2 Tablespoons
- Salt – 1 Teaspoon
- Butter – 1 Stick, sliced
- Worcestershire Sauce – 1 Cup
- Butter Cooking Spray

Let us get to cooking!

1) Preheat oven to 400°F. Place chicken in a 9"x13"x2" baking pan.
2) Combine the Season 17 and lemon pepper, sprinkle over the butter.
3) Stuff the seasoned butter sliced under the skin of the chicken.
4) Lightly season the top of the chicken with lemon pepper.
5) Spray the chicken with the butter cooking spray.
6) Pour the Worcestershire Sauce in the pan.
7) Cover the chicken with foil, bake for 30 minutes. Remove the foil, bake another 30 – 40 minutes. Periodically, spread the drippings over the chicken.
8) Let the chicken rest 15 minutes before serving. Enjoy

Baked Fried Chicken Wings

Total Minutes: 1 Hour 25 Minutes
Prep Time: 20 Minutes
Cook Time: 1 Hour 5 Minutes
Servings: 4

Ingredients

- Chicken Wings - 12
- Flour – 3/4 Cups
- Lemon Pepper – 2 Teaspoons
- Onion Powder – 2 Teaspoons
- Garlic Powder – 2 Teaspoons
- Salt – 1/2 Teaspoon
- Olive Oil to coat chicken
- Butter – 1 Stick, thinly sliced

Let us get to cooking!

1) Preheat oven to 400ºF
2) Combine the flour, lemon pepper, onion powder, garlic powder and salt in a gallon size plastic bag.
3) Coat the chicken wings with olive oil.
4) Place the chicken wings in the bag a few pieces at a time. Shake the bag until chicken is well coated.
5) Place the coated chicken in a lightly greased 9”x13”x2” baking pan.
6) Put the sliced butter on top of the chicken wings. Approximately 3 thin slices per chicken wing.
7) Cover the chicken with foil, bake for 30 minutes.
8) Remove the foil, bake another 35 minutes.
9) Enjoy!

Spicy Black Bean Quesadillas

Total Minutes: 30 Minutes
Prep Time: 20 Minutes
Cook Time: 10 Minutes
Servings: 6

Ingredients

- Olive Oil – 2 Tablespoons
- Onion – 1, Sliced
- Bell Pepper – 1, Sliced
- Black Beans – 2 15oz Cans
- Zucchini – 2, Shredded
- Spinach – 1 Cup, Chopped
- Frozen or Can Corn – 2 Cups
- Cheddar Cheese – 2 Cups
- Cayenne Pepper – ½ Teaspoon
- Black Pepper – ½ Teaspoon
- Whole Wheat Tortillas – 6 Medium Sized
- Fresh Parsley – ½ Cup Chopped
- Fresh Cilantro – ½ Chopped

Let us get to cooking!

1) In a medium 9.5-inch fry pan, heat the olive oil over medium to high heat.
2) Add the onions, bell peppers and zucchini, cook until tender. Add the spinach and black beans, cook until heated through. Add the corn, cook until heated through.
3) Add the seasonings, cayenne pepper and black pepper. Stir to combine. Remove from heat.
4) Layout the tortillas. On one side of the tortillas evenly add cheese, fresh parsley, and cilantro. Add the black bean mix on top of the cheese, add additional cheese on top of the black bean mix. Toast both sides of the tortilla in a 9.5-inch fry pan until the cheese has melted. or pre-heat the oven at 350ºF degrees. Lay the stuffed tortillas on a lightly greased baking sheet. Bake 5-7 minutes or until the cheese has melted. Enjoy!

Alaskan Crab & Lobster Pizza

Total Minutes: 3 Hours
Prep Time: 2 Hours 30 Minutes
Cook Time: 30 Minutes
Servings: 8

Wheat Pizza Crust
Ingredients

- All-Purpose Flour – 3 ½ Cups
- Granulated Sugar - 1 Teaspoon
- Instant Dry Yeast – 1
- Salt – 1 Teaspoon
- Water – 1 ¼ Cup, Warm
- Olive Oil – 2 Teaspoons

Ingredients for Pizza Sauce

- Tomato Paste - 1 (6 Ounce) Can
- Water – 6 Tablespoons
- Parmesan Cheese - 3 Tablespoons, Grated
- Minced Garlic – 1 Teaspoon
- Sugar – 2 Tablespoons
- 3/4 Teaspoon Onion Powder 1 Teaspoon
- Oregano - 1/4 Teaspoon
- Marjoram - 1/4 Teaspoon
- Ground Black Pepper - 1/4 Teaspoon

Pizza Toppings
Ingredients

- Mozzarella Cheese – 1 Bag
- Sharp Cheddar Cheese - Optional
- Lobster Tail – 1, Chopped
- Alaskan Crab Meat– 1 Cluster, Meat Removed
- Bell Peppers – Small Diced
- Black Olives – Sliced
- Green Olives - Sliced

Pizza Crust - Let us get to cooking!

1) In a large bowl, combine all dry Ingredients. Add water. Mix into dough ball.
2) Place dough onto a floured surface. Knead until dough becomes smooth, about 10 minutes. Place dough into a bowl greased with olive oil. Rotate the dough ball to coat with the olive oil. Cover with a kitchen towel, sit in a warm place, about 1 hour.
3) After the dough has risen, place on a floured surface. Cut the dough in half for thin pizza crust or use entire ball for a thicker crust. Roll the dough again into a tighter ball and let rise another hour and doubled in size.

Pizza Sauce - Let us get to cooking!

In a small bowl, mix all ingredients together. Set aside.

Time to Assemble

1) Preheat the oven to 425 F
2) Roll the dough into a large circle with a rolling pin, about ¼ inch. Place on an oiled pizza pan or cookie sheet. Spread the pizza sauce on top. Add mozzarella cheese, top with other topping ingredients. Bake for 10 to 15 minutes until the crust is golden brown around the edges and cheese is melted on the top.

Wheat Veggie Pizza

Wheat Veggie Pizza Ingredients

Follow Process for the Alaskan Crab and Lobster Pizza

Use wheat flour instead of all-purpose flour.

Ingredients

- Black Olives – 4- 5 Sliced
- Green Olives – 4-5 Sliced
- Cherry Tomatoes – 4- 5 Slices
- Red Onion – ¼ Large Sliced
- Bell Peppers – ¼ Chopped
- Asparagus – 4-5

Shrimp Alfredo

Total Minutes: 45 Minutes
Prep Time: 30 Minutes
Cook Time: 15 Minutes
Servings: 4

Homemade Pasta
Ingredients (Or store-bought pasta- follow instructions on box)

- All Purpose Flour - 3 Cups
- Parsley Flakes –2 Tablespoons
- Eggs – 4 Beaten
- Olive Oil – 2 Teaspoon
- Salt – 2 Teaspoon
- Water – 5 Cups of water

Pasta - Let us get to cooking.

1) Place flour in a large bowl. Make a well, add the eggs, parsley flakes, olive oil and salt.
2) Massage the Ingredients together. If the dough is dry, wet your hands and continue to massage the dough. Massage until the dough comes together.
3) Shape the dough into a ball.
4) Roll the dough onto a lightly floured surface with the rolling pin, about 1/16 inch.
5) Use a knife to cut the dough into strips about 1/8 of an inch. Or use a pasta roller if you have one.
6) To prevent the pasta strips from sticking, dust with flour. Set aside.

Shrimp Ingredients

- Uncooked Shrimp, deveined - 1 pound medium sized
- Butter – ½ Stick
- Olive Oil - 2 tablespoons
- Minced Garlic - 2 tablespoons
- Lemon Pepper - 2 tablespoon

Shrimp - Let us get to cooking.

1) In a 3-quart sauté pan, melt butter, add olive oil and minced garlic, cook until garlic is aromatic.
2) Add the shrimp, 2 tablespoons of fresh or 1 tablespoon of dried parsley and lemon pepper. Cook and stir until shrimp turns pink. Set aside.

Alfredo Sauce
Ingredients

- Cream Cheese - 1 8oz Block, softened
- Heavy Cream – ½ Cup
- Water - ½ Cup
- Butter – 4 Tablespoons
- Minced Garlic – 2 Tablespoons
- Parmesan Cheese (Freshly Grated) – 2 Cups
- Lemon Pepper – 1 Tablespoons
- Salt to Taste
- Freshly Ground Pepper to Taste
- Fresh or Dried Parsley Flakes as Needed

Alfredo Sauce - Let us get to cooking.

1) In a 3-quart sauté pan, melt the butter and cream cheese under medium to low heat. Add the water, stir until combined. Reduce heat and let simmer for 2 minutes.
2) Add the parmesan cheese, stir as it melts into a creamy sauce. Add more water if necessary.
3) Season to taste fresh ground black pepper. Toss with the hot cooked pasta and shrimp. Sprinkle with parsley flakes and parmesan cheese. Enjoy.

Southern Eggrolls

Total Minutes: 40 Minutes
Prep Time: 20 Minutes
Cook Time: 20 Minutes
Servings: 4

Ingredients

- Olive Oil – 3 tablespoons
- Onion – 1 medium sized, chopped
- Minced Garlic – 1 teaspoon
- Bell Peppers – 1 chopped
- Ground Chicken – 1 pound
- Lemon Pepper – 1 teaspoon
- Salt to taste
- Egg Rolls Wrappers
- Cooked Spinach or greens
- Cooked Yellow or Brown Rice
- Mozzarella or Cheddar Cheese
- Vegetable Oil for deep frying

Let us get to cooking!

1. Heat the oil in 3-quart sauté pan under medium to high heat.
2. Add the onions, minced garlic, and bell peppers to the skillet. Cook until onions and bell peppers are tender.
3. Add the ground chicken, cook until browned.
4. Add the lemon pepper.
5. Salt to taste.
6. Layout the egg roll wrappers, in the middle of the wrapper crosswise, leaving about an inch on each side, layer with the spinach or green, rice, cheese and about 2 tablespoons of the ground chicken.
7. Fold over the filling halfway, tuck under the filling, fold the left and right corners of the wrapper to the middle of the roll, dip your fingers in the water to line the outer inner edge of the last corner to "glue" the egg roll together. Roll tightly.
8. Deep Fry 4-5 at a time for 1 – 2 minutes, until golden brown. Remove the eggs rolls to a paper towels to drain the excess oil. Enjoy

Pan Seared Tilapia

Total Minutes: **25 Minutes**
Prep Time: **15 Minutes**
Cook Time: **10 Minutes**
Servings: **4**

Ingredients

- Olive Oil, 6 Tablespoons
- Tilapia, 4 Filets
- Lemon – 1, Sliced
- Butter - 4 Tablespoons, Sliced
- Lemon Pepper - 2 Tablespoons
- Garlic Powder - 1 Tablespoons
- Onion Powder - 1 Tablespoons
- Black Pepper- 1 Tablespoons
- Old Bay Seasoning - 1 Tablespoons
- Salt to Taste

Let us get to cooking!

1) In a 9.5-inch fry pan, heat 3 tablespoons of olive oil over medium heat.
2) Lay the filets in the pan.
3) Coat the filets with the remaining Olive Oil
4) Place a slice of lemon on top of each filet.
5) Add a slice of butter on top of the lemon.
6) Sprinkle the seasoning, lemon pepper, garlic powder, onion, powder, black pepper, and old bay seasoning on top.
7) Cook until the filets turn white and golden brown on the edges.
8) Another option would be to bake in the oven on a lightly greased baking sheet for 10-15 minutes. Broil the last few minutes for a golden-brown top of the filet.
9) Salt to taste if needed. Enjoy!

Grilled Cheddar Cheese Chicken Sandwich

Total Minutes: **25 Minutes**
Prep Time: **15 Minutes**
Cook Time: **10 Minutes**
Servings: **2**

Ingredients

- Butter – 4 Tablespoons, softened
- Shredded Cheddar Cheese – 2 Cups
- Cooked Chicken Breast – 2, pulled or chopped
- Fresh Cilantro
- Butter Cooking Spray

Let us get to cooking.

1) Heat a 9.5inch fry pan. Coat the pan with the butter cooking spray.
2) Generously butter one side of the bread. Place bread butter-side-down onto the fry pan.
3) Top with cheddar cheese, chicken, and the cilantro. Add more cheese on top of the Cilantro.
4) Butter the second place on top, then flip to toast the second piece of bread. Repeat for the second sandwich. Enjoy.

Roasted Garlic Speckled Perch

Total Minutes: 30 Minutes
Prep Time: 10 Minutes
Cook Time: 20 Minutes
Servings: 2

Ingredients

- Speckled Perch – 2 Large
- Roasted Garlic Seasoning – 2 Tablespoons
- Lemon Pepper – 1 Tablespoon
- Salt – ¼ Tablespoon
- Butter – 4 Tablespoon, sliced
- Baking Spray

Let us get to cooking!

1) Preheat oven to 400°F
2) Combine the roasted garlic seasoning and lemon pepper and salt. Season Speckled Perch on both sides.
3) Place fish in an oil coasted 9"x13"x2" baking pan.
4) Put the sliced butter on top of the fish.
5) Cover the fish with foil, bake for 10 minutes.
6) Remove the foil, bake another 10 minutes. Enjoy.

Brown Butter Bacon Lobster Tail

Total Minutes:	25 Minutes
Prep Time:	10 Minutes
Cook Time:	10 Minutes
Servings:	2

Ingredients

- Lobster Tail - 2
- Butter – ½ Stick
- Bacon Grease – ¼ Cup
- Lemon Pepper – ½ Teaspoon
- Onion Powder – ½ Teaspoon
- Garlic Powder – ½ Teaspoon

Let us get to cooking!

1) Slice the top of the lobster tail down the middle. Place a knife on top and press down firmly. Tip: Place the lobster on a paper towel to reduce the movement while cutting.

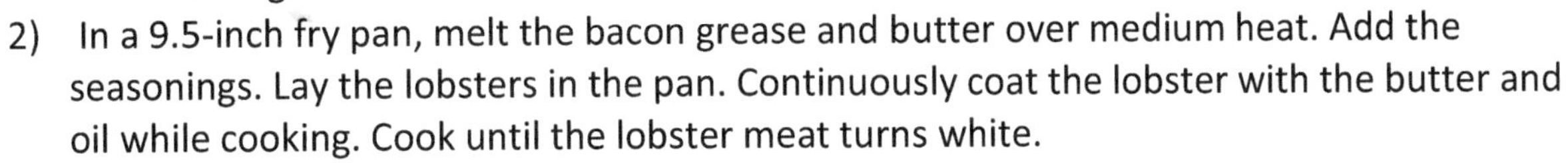

2) In a 9.5-inch fry pan, melt the bacon grease and butter over medium heat. Add the seasonings. Lay the lobsters in the pan. Continuously coat the lobster with the butter and oil while cooking. Cook until the lobster meat turns white.
3) Place a slice of lemon on top of each filet. Enjoy!

Curry Chicken

Total Minutes: 45 Minutes
Prep Time: 20 Minutes
Cook Time: 25 Minutes
Servings: 4

Ingredients

- Cooked White or Brown Rice
- Olive Oil - 3 Tablespoons
- Onion - 1 Medium, Diced
- Minced Garlic – 2 Tablespoons
- Parsley Flakes – 2 Tablespoons
- Onion Powder – 2 Tablespoons
- Cumin – 1 Teaspoon
- Red Pepper – 1 Teaspoon
- Curry Powder - 3 Tablespoons
- Chicken Breasts – 1 Lb., Cut into Cubes
- Flour – ¼ Cup
- Heavy Cream – 1 ½ Cups
- Chicken Stock - ½ Cup
- Marsala Wine - ½ Cup
- Salt to Taste
- Freshly Ground Black Pepper – 1 Teaspoon

Let us get to cooking!

1) In a 3-quart sauté pan, heat the oil on medium to high heat, add onions and minced garlic, cook until translucent.
2) Add parsley flakes, onion powder, cumin, red pepper, curry powder, let toast for 1 minute.
3) Add the chicken, cook until the chicken turns white.
4) Add the flour, cook until blend with the other ingredients.
5) Add the heavy cream, chicken stock, marsala wine. Let simmer on low for 10 minutes.
6) Serve over white or brown rice.

Meaty Lasagna

Total Minutes: 1 Hour 30 Minutes
Prep Time: 45 Minutes
Cook Time: 45 Minutes
Servings: 12

Ingredients

- 12 Lasagna Noodles, Cooked
- Thyme- 3 Tablespoons
- Dried Basil -3 Tablespoons
- Crush Rose Mary - 3 Tablespoons
- Italian Seasoning- 3 Tablespoons
- Onion Powder – 3 Tablespoons
- Lemon Pepper– 3 Tablespoons
- Garlic Powder– 3 Tablespoons
- Olive Oil – 3 Tablespoons
- Onion – 1 Large, Chopped
- Bell Pepper – 1, Chopped
- Spaghetti Sauce – 2 Jars (24 Ounce)
- Zucchini – 1 Sliced
- Spinach – 1 Small Bag
- Ground Chuck 1 ½ Lbs.
- 2 1/2 Mozzarella Cheese – 3 Cups
- 1 (15 Ounce) Ricotta Cheese – 1 15-Ounce Container
- 1/2 Cup Cheddar Cheese – 3 Cups

Let us get to cooking.

1) Combine the seasonings, thyme, dried basil, crushed rosemary, Italian seasoning, onion, powder, lemon pepper and garlic powder. Set aside.
2) Add olive oil to a 3-quart sauté' pan under medium heat.
3) Sautee Onions and Bell Peppers
4) Add Spaghetti Sauce and 3 tablespoons of the seasoning mix.
5) In another 3-quart sauté pan, brown the ground chuck over medium heat. Drain the excess oil.

Meaty Lasagna Continued:

6) Add the ground chuck to the pot with the spaghetti sauce, add 3 tablespoons of the seasoning mix. Let simmer on low for 30 minutes.
7) Place the ricotta cheese in a bowl, add 3 tablespoons of the seasoning mix. Set aside.
8) Pre-heat oven to 350ºF
9) In a 9" x 9"x2" baking pan, spread some of the sauce onto the bottom of the pan to prevent sticking.
10) Layer 3 – 4 of the cooked lasagna noodles, layer 1/3 of the sauce, layer 1/3 of the ricotta mix, layer 1/3 of the mozzarella cheese, layer the spinach and zucchini. Repeat two more times.
11) Top with mozzarella and cheddar cheese. Cover with foil. Bake 30 minutes, then remove the foil. Bake an additional 30 minutes or until heated through and bubbling.
12) Let stand 15-20 minutes before cutting into squares.

Southerly Style Chicken & Dumplings

Total Minutes: 1 Hour 45 Minutes
Prep Time: 30 Minutes
Cook Time: 1 Hour 15 Minutes
Servings: 8

Chicken and Broth

Ingredients

- Raw Chicken Breast - 3
- Water- 6 Cups
- Celery Juice – 6 Cups
- Salt – ½ Teaspoon
- Bell Pepper – 1, Chopped
- Celery – 1 Stalk, Small Dice
- Onion – Medium Sized, Small Dice
- Carrots – 2 Sliced
- Poultry Seasoning – ½ Tablespoon
- Ground Thyme – ½ Teaspoon
- Chicken Bullions – 3 Small
- Salt to Taste
- Fresh Ground Pepper to Taste

Dumplings Ingredients

- All-Purpose Flour – 1 ¾ Cups
- Baking Powder - 1 Teaspoons
- Salt - ½ Teaspoon
- Parsley Flakes – 1 Tablespoon
- Onion Powder – 1 Tablespoon
- Cold Butter – 5 Tablespoons small dice.
- Milk – 1/2 Cup

Southerly Style Chicken & Dumplings Continued:

Chicken Broth - Let us get to cooking!

1) In a 6-quart stockpot, place all ingredients.
2) Bring to a boil.
3) Remove the scum off the surface with a slotted spoon.
4) Simmer broth over medium to high heat until chicken is done, about 1 hour.
5) While chicken is cooking, make the dumplings.
6) Remove chicken from the pot with slotted spoon; let cool. Pull apart! Set aside.

Dumplings - Let us get to cooking.

1) In a medium sized bowl, sift together flour, baking powder, salt.
2) Add chilled butter to the flour mixture. Gently massage with your hands (use gloves or not)
3) Place dough onto a cleaned floured surface and lightly knead. Using a rolling pin, lightly roll dough out to ¼ inch thickness.
4) Cut dough into desired shape. Set aside.

Time to Assemble

1) Return the broth to a simmer, add the dumplings. Cook, stirring occasionally, until tender, about 15 – 20 minutes. The broth will start to thicken.
2) Add the pulled chicken to the pot; cook about 5 minutes.
3) Enjoy!

Rosemary & Lemon Pepper Chicken

Total Minutes:	30 Minutes
Prep Time:	20 Minutes
Cook Time:	10 Minutes
Servings:	4 to 6

Ingredients

- Olive Oil – ½ Cup
- Butter – 4 Tablespoons
- Fresh Rosemary – 2 Sprigs, Chopped
- Lemon Pepper – 2 Teaspoons
- Chicken Breast – 4 To 6. Large Chicken Breast Should Be Sliced Vertically
- Salt to Taste

Let us get to cooking!

1) Pour olive oil and place butter in a 9.5-inch fry pan over medium to high heat.
2) After the butter has melted add the rosemary and lemon pepper.
3) Once the rosemary becomes aromatic, add the chicken.
4) Cook until golden brown on both sides. The internal temperature should be 165 F.
5) Enjoy.

Chicken Pot Pie

Crust Total Minutes:	1 Hour 45 Minutes
Prep Time:	1 Hour 15 Minutes
Cook Time:	30 Minutes
Servings:	4

Crust Ingredients

- All Purpose Flour 2 ½ Cups
- Salt 1 Teaspoon
- Cold Butter - 1 ½ Sticks, Grated
- Cold Water ¼ Cup
- Egg – 1 (for Egg Wash)

Filling Ingredients

- Olive Oil – 4 Tablespoons
- Butter - 4 Tablespoons
- Onions – 1 Medium Sized
- Bell Peppers – ½ Chopped
- Minced Garlic – 1 Teaspoon
- Onion Powder – 1 Tablespoon
- Garlic Powder – 1 Tablespoon
- Poultry Season – 1 Teaspoon
- Lemon Pepper – 1 Teaspoon
- Chicken Breast – 2, Cut into Small Pieces
- Flour – ½ Cup
- Chicken Broth – 3 Cups
- Frozen Mix Vegetables – 1 Small Bag
- Salt to Taste

Chicken Pot Pie Continued:

Let us get crusting.

1) In a large bowl, sift together flour and salt.
2) Add chilled butter to the flour mixture. Gently massage with your hands.
3) Add cold water. Add more if the dough is dry.
4) Place dough onto a cleaned floured surface and lightly knead for 5 minutes.
5) Roll the dough in a ball, wrap with plastic wrap or place in a plastic bag. Chill for 30 minutes.
6) In the meantime, make the filling.

Let us get to cooking the Chicken Filling

1. In a 3-quart sauté' pan heat the butter and olive oil. Add the onions, peppers, garlic. cook until soft.
2. Add chicken – season with onion powder, garlic powder, poultry seasoning, and lemon pepper.
3. Cook until the chicken turns white.
4. Add flour, stir in with other Ingredients. Cook until flour is golden brown.
5. Add broth and frozen veggies
6. Let simmer until gravy thickens.
7. Add salt to taste.

Time to assemble

1. Pre-heat the oven to 350°F.
2. Cut dough in half. Using a rolling pin, lightly roll dough out to ¼ inch thickness. Make sure the dough will cover the 9" x 9" x 2" pie pan. Repeat for the top layer.
3. Place the dough in the pie pan, press against the side of the pan. Cut the excess dough to the size of the pie pan.
4. Add the filling.
5. Place the top layer of dough, again, cut the excess dough that is overlapping to the size of the pie pan. Pinch the two layers of dough together. Cut slices into the top layer for venting.
6. Crack the egg into a small bowl, add 1 tablespoon of water. Mix well for the egg wash. Using a basting brush, coat the top of the pie crust with the egg wash to make the crush shine.
7. Bake for 45 minutes to an hour. Enjoy.

Ground Chuck Stew

Total Minutes:	**50 Minutes**
Prep Time:	**20 Minutes**
Cook Time:	**30 Minutes**
Servings:	**8**

Ingredients

- Cooked White Rice – 6-8 servings
- Ground Chuck – 1 Lb.
- Olive Oil – 3 Tablespoons
- Onion – I Medium Sized Onion, Diced Small
- Bell Peppers – 1, Diced Small
- Crushed Tomatoes – 2 15oz Cans
- Frozen Corn – 1 Medium Sized Bag
- Lemon Pepper – 1 Tablespoon
- Fresh Ground Pepper – 1 Tablespoon
- Garlic Powder – 1 Tablespoon
- Onion Powder – 1 Tablespoon
- Salt to taste

Let us get to cooking!

1. In a 6-quart stockpot, brown the ground chuck, drain off the excess grease. Set aside in a bowl.
2. Using the same stockpot heat the olive under medium heat.
3. Add the chopped onions and bell peppers. Cook until onion is tender and lightly browned.
4. Add the ground chuck back to the saucepan.
5. Add the crushed tomatoes and corn.
6. Add the Lemon Pepper, Garlic Powder and Onion powder.
7. Salt to taste.
8. Cover, and let simmer for 30 minutes.
9. Serve over the white rice.

Sour Pepper Chicken Wings

Total Minutes: 1 Hour 10 Minutes
Prep Time: 10 Minutes
Cook Time: 1 Hour
Servings: 4

Ingredients

- Chicken Wings – 12 Pack
- Butter – 1 Stick, Melted
- Lemon Pepper – 2 Tablespoons

Let us get to cooking!

1) Place the chicken wings in a 9" x 9" x 2" Baking Pan.
2) Bake for 1 hour
3) In a large bowl with a lid, add the butter and lemon pepper. Stir to combine
4) Add the hot cooked wings, cover the bowl with the lid and shake, shake, shake.
5) Enjoy.

Fiery Hot Wings

Ingredients

- Chicken Wings – 12 pack
- Butter – 1 stick, melted
- Hot Sauce – ½ Cup

Let us get to cooking!

1) Place the chicken wings in a 9" x 9" x 2" Baking Pan.
2) Bake for 1 hour
3) In a large bowl with a lid, add the butter and hot sauce. Stir to combine
4) Add the hot cooked wings, cover the bowl with the lid and shake, shake, shake. Enjoy.

Turkey Bell Peppers

Total Minutes: 1 Hour 5 Minutes
Prep Time: 30 Minutes
Cook Time: 30-35 Minutes
Servings: 5

Ingredients

- Bell Peppers - 5, variety of colors
- Ground Turkey – 1lb
- Olive Oil – 7 tablespoons
- Medium Onion – 1 chopped
- minced garlic – 1 teaspoon
- Roma Tomatoes – 1 cup diced
- Oregano – 1 teaspoon
- Dried Parsley – 1 teaspoon
- Lemon Pepper – 1 teaspoon
- Ground Thyme – ½ teaspoon
- Cayenne – ½ teaspoon
- Cooked Brown Rice – 2 cups
- Salt to taste
- Pepper to taste
- Pepper Jack Cheese – 2 Cups

Let us get to cooking

1) Slice the top off and core the bell peppers, remove the seeds and membranes. Wash, dry and coat the outside with olive oil and set aside.
2) Heat 3 tablespoons of olive oil in a large saucepan over medium to heat. Add the ground turkey, cook until browned. Drain the excess liquid. Set aside the meat.
3) In the same saucepan, heat 3 tablespoons of olive oil. Add the onions and minced garlic, cook until tender.
4) Preheat oven to 350ºF.
5) In a large mixing bowl, combine the ground turkey with the roma tomatoes, all the seasonings and the cooked brown rice and 1 cup of the pepper jack cheese. Mix well. Salt to and pepper to taste.
6) Stuff the bell peppers with the ground turkey mix. Top the bell peppers with the remaining pepper jack cheese. Bake in a 9" x 9" x 2" Baking Pan for 30-35 minutes.

Pan Seared Salmon Filet

Total Minutes: 50 Minutes
Prep Time: 20 Minutes
Cook Time: 30 Minutes
Servings: 2

Ingredients

- Butter – 1 Tablespoon
- Olive Oil – 2 Tablespoons
- Lemon Pepper – 1 Teaspoon
- Onion Powder – 1 Teaspoon
- Garlic Powder – 1 Teaspoon n
- Red Pepper – Pinch
- Salmon Filet - 2

Let us get to cooking!

1. In a 9.5-inch fry pan, heat the olive oil and butter over medium heat.
2. Add the dry seasoning, stir.
3. Add the filets in the pan.
4. Season the filets with the lemon pepper.
5. Cooked on each side for 2-4 Minutes or until the salmon turns pink.
6. Salt to taste if needed. Enjoy!

Baked Red Snapper

Total Minutes: 50 Minutes
Prep Time: 20 Minutes
Cook Time: 30 Minutes
Servings: 6

Ingredients

- Red Onions – 1, Sliced
- Red Snapper – 1 Whole
- Lemon Pepper – 1 Tablespoon
- Black Pepper – 1 Tablespoon
- Salt - ½ Teaspoon
- Lime – 1, 7 Slices
- Butter – ½ Stick, Sliced

Let us get to cooking!

1. Pre-heat the oven to 400ºF
2. Combine all the seasonings in one small bowl. Mix. Set aside.
3. Cover a 9" x 12" x 2" Baking Pan with a large piece of foil.
4. Lightly grease the foil with butter.
5. Layer half of the red onions on top of the foil.
6. Place the red snapper on top of the onions.
7. With a knife score the top of the red snapper. Make 4-5 crevices.
8. Sprinkle the seasonings on top of the red snapper.
9. Layer the limes, butter slices and red onions on top of seasoned Red Snapper. Lightly cover the snapper with the foil.
10. Bake covered for 20 minutes. Open the foil and broil for 10 minutes. Enjoy.

Spaghetti and Meatballs

Total Minutes: 50-60 Minutes
Prep Time: 20-30 Minutes
Cook Time: 30 Minutes
Servings: 6

Spaghetti Sauce
Ingredients

- Olive Oil – 3 Tablespoons
- Onion – 1 Large, Chopped
- Bell Peppers – 1, Chopped
- Lemon Pepper – 2 Tablespoons
- Black Pepper – 1 Teaspoons
- Onion Powder – 2 Tablespoons
- Celery – 2 Stalks, Pureed
- Minced Garlic – 1 Tablespoons
- Parsley Flakes -1 Teaspoon
- Crushed Tomatoes – 2 28oz Cans
- Sugar – 2 Tablespoons

Meatballs
Ingredients

- Chopped Onion – 1, Pureed
- Lemon Pepper – 1 Tablespoon
- Black Pepper – 1 Teaspoons
- Onion Powder – 1 Tablespoon
- Minced Garlic – 1 Teaspoon
- Ground Chuck – 1 Pound

Let us get to cooking the Spaghetti Sauce

1) In a 3-quart sauté pan, heat the olive oil.
2) Add the onions and bell peppers, cook until tender.
3) Add the lemon pepper, black pepper, onion pepper, celery, and minced garlic, stir to mix well.
4) Add the parsley flakes, crushed tomatoes, and sugar.
5) Let simmer while you prepare the meatballs or for 30 minutes.

Spaghetti Pasta -1 Box 16oz

Spaghetti Pasta -1 Box

1. Follow the instructions to cook the spaghetti

Let us get to cooking the meatballs

1) In a large bowl add all the ingredients. Mix well with your hands.
2) Form the meatballs to the size you desire. Add the meatballs to the spaghetti sauce, let cook for 30 minutes or until the meatballs are done. The internal temperature for the meatballs should be 160 F.
3) Serve the spaghetti sauce and meatball over the spaghetti pasta. Enjoy!

Smothered Cubed Steak

Total Minutes: 40 Minutes
Prep Time: 10 Minutes
Cook Time: 30 Minutes
Servings: 4 - 6
Ingredients

- Olive Oil – ½ Cup
- Cubed Steak, 4 To 6
- Onions – 1, Sliced
- Flour – 2 Cups
- Lemon Pepper – 1 Teaspoon
- Onion Powder – 1 Teaspoon
- Garlic Powder – 1 Teaspoon
- Water, Beef Stock or Chicken Stock – 2 – 3 Cups
- Salt to Taste
- Pepper to Taste

Let us get to cooking!

1) In a medium sized bowl add the flour, lemon pepper, onion powder and garlic powder. Set aside.
2) Heat a 3-quart sauté pan over medium-high heat.
3) Coat the steaks with the seasoned flour. Sear the cubed steaks on both sides until browned. Remove the cubed steaks to a baking pan. Set aside.
4) Add the onions to the same pan to sauté. Add a little more oil if needed.
5) Cook the onions until tender. Add 3 tablespoons of the remaining seasoned flour to the pan. Cook until brown. Stir continuously to prevent burning the flour.
6) Add 2 to 3 cups of chicken broth or water, stir until blended with the roux.
7) Add the cubed steaks back to the pan.
8) Salt and pepper to taste.
9) Let simmer on low for 20 minutes. Enjoy with rice or mashed potatoes.

Gourmet Burgers

Total Minutes: 35 Minutes
Prep Time: 15 Minutes
Cook Time: 20 Minutes
Servings: 6 - 8

Ingredients

- Ground Chuck – 2 Lbs.
- Ground Sausage - 1 Lb.
- Onion Powder – 1 Tablespoon
- Red Pepper – ½ Teaspoon
- Lemon Powder – 1 Tablespoon
- Onion Powder – 1 Tablespoon
- Fresh Ground Pepper – 1 Teaspoon
- Pickled Jalapeno – ½ Cup
- Minced Garlic – ¼ Cup
- Crumbled Blue Cheese – 1 Cup

Let us get to cooking!

1. In a large bowl, combine all the ingredients.
2. With gloved hands mix the ingredients well.
3. Scoop some of the mixture into your hands. Enough to make the size of a baseball or choose the size you want.
4. Place the burgers on the grill, press down to flatten. Cook the burgers until the internal temperature is 160°F for well done or 145°F for medium well.
5. Enjoy with your favorite burger buns and toppings.

Garlic Shrimp & Savory Cheddar Cheese

Total Minutes: 55 Minutes
Prep Time: 30 Minutes
Cook Time: 25 Minutes
Servings: 4-5

Ingredients for Grits

- Grits – 4-5 Serving
- Milk – ¼ Cup
- Butter – 2 Tablespoons
- Cheddar Cheese – 2 Cups
- Pickled Jalapeno Peppers – ¼ Cup, Diced
- Onion – 1 Small, Finely Chopped
- Bell Peppers – ½ Cup, Chopped
- Salt to taste

Let us get to cooking the Grits.

1) Follow the instructions on the bag to cook the grits.
2) Add ¼ cup of milk and butter, stir to mix well.
3) Add the cheddar cheese, stir to mix well
4) Add the pickled jalapeno peppers, onions, and bell peppers. Stir to mix well.
5) Salt to taste

Ingredients for Garlic Shrimp

- Butter – 4 Tablespoons
- Onions – 1, Chopped
- Minced Garlic – 1 Teaspoon
- Raw Shrimp – 40 Medium Sized, Deveined, Shelled
- Lemon Pepper – 1 Teaspoon
- Cayenne Pepper – Pinch

Let us get to cooking! for Shrimp

1) In a 9.5" fry pan, melt butter under medium heat.
2) Add the onions and minced garlic, cook until onions are tender.
3) Add the shrimp and seasonings, lemon pepper and cayenne pepper.
4) Cook until the shrimp turns pink.
5) Serve over the savory cheddar cheese grits. Enjoy

Shrimp Fried Brown Rice

Total Minutes: 50 Minutes
Prep Time: 15 Minutes
Cook Time: 35 Minutes
Servings: 4

Ingredients

- Olive Oil as needed
- Onions – ½ Cup, chopped
- Carrots – Shredded, 1 10oz bag
- Frozen Sweet Peas, 1 12oz bag
- Raw Shrimp, 20 mediums sized, deveined, shelled.
- Cooked Brown Rice, 4 cups
- Eggs – 2
- Green Onions – ½ cup, diced
- Soy Sauce – as needed

Let us get to cooking

1) In a 3-quart sauté pan or wok heat 3 tablespoons of olive oil under medium to high heat.
2) Add the onions cook until tender
3) Add the carrots and peas, cook until heated through.
4) Add the shrimp, cook until the shrimp turns pink.
5) Add the cooked brown rice (add more oil if needed) cook until toasted.
6) Crack the eggs over the rice, stir and toss until the eggs are cooked.
7) Add the green onions, cook until heated.
8) Enjoy with soy sauce.

Braised Pork Chops

Total Minutes: 35 Minutes
Prep Time: 10 Minutes
Cook Time: 25 Minutes
Servings: 4 - 6

Ingredients

- Pork Chops – 4 to 6 pork chops
- Lemon Pepper – 1 teaspoon
- Onion Powder – 1 teaspoon
- Garlic Powder – 1 teaspoon
- Vegetable Oil – 1/4 Cup
- Flour – ½ Cup
- Rose Mary - 2-4 Sprigs
- Chicken Stock – 2 Cups
- Worcestershire Sauce - ½ Cup

Let us get to cooking!

1) Pre-Heat the oven to 400 F.
2) Combine the lemon pepper, onion powder, garlic powder, salt, and pepper with the flour. Flour the pork chops.
3) Heat the oil in an oven-safe 9.5-inch fry pan over medium-high heat. Cook the pork chops on each side for about 2 minutes each.
4) Add the chicken stock and Worcestershire Sauce. Place the Rosemary Spring on top of the pork chops.
5) Place the oven-safe fry pan in the oven, bake for 15 - 20 minutes. Enjoy

Southwestern Brandy Chili

Total Minutes:	**50 Minutes**
Prep Time:	**20 Minutes**
Cook Time:	**30 Minutes**
Servings:	**4 - 6**

Ingredients

- Ground Chuck 1 ½ - 2 Pounds
- Olive Oil – 3 Tablespoons
- Red Onion – ½ Chopped
- Small Sweet Peppers – 3 chopped
- Minced Garlic – 2 Tablespoons
- Chili Powder – 2.5oz Bottle
- Lemon Pepper – 3 Tablespoons
- Onion Powder - 3 Tablespoons
- Garlic Powder - 3 Tablespoons
- Ground Pepper - 3 Tablespoons
- Brandy – ½ Cup
- Tomato Sauce 3 - 29 oz can
- Soy Sauce 3 Tablespoons
- Sugar – 2 Tablespoons
- Dark Kidney Bean – 1 Can 15.50oz
- Black Beans – 1 can 15.25oz
- Whole Sweet Kernel Corn -1 frozen bag 32oz
- Salt to taste

Let us get to cooking

1) In a 6-quart stockpot, brown the ground chuck. Drain the excess oil, set aside the ground chuck in a bowl.
2) In the same stockpot, heat the olive oil under medium to high heat. Cook the red onions and bell peppers until tender. Toss in the minced garlic, lemon pepper, onion powder, garlic powder and ground pepper. Cook for 1 minute.
3) Add the brandy, tomato sauce, soy sauce and sugar. Stir to mix well. Add the dark kidney beans, black beans, and corn. Mix well. Add the cooked ground chuck, turn down the heat to low to medium, salt to taste and let simmer for 30 minutes. Enjoy!

Tender Sirloin Tips

Total Minutes: 35 Minutes
Prep Time: 10 Minutes
Cook Time: 25 Minutes
Servings: 4 - 6

Ingredients

- Vegetable Oil - 2 Tablespoons
- Onion – ½ Cup, Sliced
- Bell Pepper – 1, sliced
- Minced Garlic – 1 Teaspoon
- Salt - 1 Teaspoon Salt
- Freshly Ground Pepper – Pinch
- Sirloin Steak - 1 Lb., Sliced Thinly
    - (Tip: Freeze, Thew Slightly, Cut with A Knife)
- Butter – 2 Teaspoons
- Flour – ½ Cup
- Chicken Bouillon – 1 Small
- Water – ¾ Cup
- Soy Sauce -2 Tablespoons
- Steak Sauce – 2 Tablespoons

Let us get to cooking.

1) Heat the vegetable oil in a 3-quart sauté pan. Add the onions, bell pepper and minced garlic. Cook until the veggies are tender.
2) Add the Sirloin tips, lightly season with the salt and pepper. Cook until browned. Remove from the pan. Set aside.
3) Melt the butter and add the flour to the pan under low to medium heat, cook until dark brown, but not burnt.
4) Add the water, chicken bouillon, soy sauce and steak sauce. Add the steak back to the pan. Cook until the gravy thickens.
5) Enjoy over rice or mashed potatoes.

Meaty Meatloaf

Total Minutes: 1 Hour 10 Minutes
Prep Time: 20 Minutes
Cook Time: 50 Minutes
Servings: 6-8

Ingredients

- Ground Chuck – 1 ½ - 2 Pounds
- Onion – 1 Finely Chopped
- Bell Pepper 1 Finely Chopped
- Breadcrumbs - 1 Cup
- Ketchup - ½ Cup
- Egg - 1
- Worcestershire Sauce – ¼ Cup
- Steak Sauce – ½ Cup
- Salt – ½ Teaspoon
- Freshly Ground Pepper – ½ Teaspoon
- Barbeque Sauce – ½ Cup

Let us get to cooking

1) Pre-heat the oven to 400ºF. In a large bowl, mix all the ingredients except for the barbeque sauce. Mix well.
2) Place the ground chuck mixture in a 9" x 9" x 2" Baking Pan. Shape into a bread loaf. Cover the pan with foil.
3) Bake for 30 minutes, then add the barbeque sauce on top. Bake an addition 20 minutes. The internal temperature should be 160ºF. Enjoy.

Sides

Tasty Cabbage

Total Minutes: 35 Minutes
Prep Time: 15 Minutes
Cook Time: 20 Minutes
Servings: 6-8
Ingredients

- Bacon - 5 Stripes or Half Cup of Bacon Grease
- Onion – 1, Sliced or Chopped
- Bell Pepper – 1, Sliced or Chopped
- Celery - 2 Stalks, Chopped
- Cabbage- 1 Head, Chopped
- Apple Vinegar - 1/2 Cup
- Water - 2 Cups
- Chicken Bullions – 3 Small

Let us get to cooking!

1. Heat a 6-quart stockpot over medium-high heat.
2. Cook the bacon or add the bacon grease.
3. When the grease is hot or bacon is done, add the onions, bell peppers and celery, cook until the veggies are soft.
4. Add the vinegar, water, and chicken bullions. Let the liquids come to a simmer.
5. Add the cabbage and stir to coat with the liquids. Reduce the heat to low, cover, and cook until the vegetables are tender, about 20 minutes.
6. Uncover and stir periodically. Add more water if needed. Cook another 5-10 minutes.
7. For a more tender texture cook until veggies turn light brown.
8. Salt to taste.
9. Enjoy

Eggplant & Corn Dish

Total Minutes: 15 Minutes
Prep Time: 10 Minutes
Cook Time: 5 Minutes
Servings: 4

Ingredients

- Olive Oil – 3 Tablespoons
- Butter – 3 Tablespoons
- Onion – 1 Small, Diced
- Bell Pepper – ½ Cup, Chopped
- Eggplant – 1 Medium Sized
- Frozen Corn – 1 Medium Sized Bag
- Lemon Pepper – 1 teaspoon
- Salt to taste

Let us get to cooking!

1. In a 9.5" fry pan, heat the olive oil and butter.
2. Add the onions and bell peppers, cook until tender.
3. Add the eggplant, cook until tender.
4. Add the corn, cook until heated through.
5. Season with the lemon pepper and salt to taste.
6. Enjoy.

Russet Mashed Potatoes

Total Minutes: **1 Hour**
Prep Time: **20 Minutes**
Cook Time: **40 Minutes**
Servings: **5**

Ingredients

- Russet Potatoes – 5 To 6, Chopped
- Water as Needed
- Milk – 2 Cups (More for a Looser Mash Potatoes)
- Butter – 4 Tablespoons
- Heavy Cream – ½ Cup
- Cheddar or Parmesan Cheese – 1 Cup, Optional
- Salt to Taste
- Pepper to Taste

Let us get to cooking!

1) In a 3-quart sauté pan place the potatoes and enough water to cover the potatoes.
2) Under medium to high heat cook the potatoes until tender.
3) Drain the water off the potatoes.
4) Using a potato masher (blender or strainer), mash the potatoes.
5) Add the butter and heavy cream. Mix well.
6) Add the cheese, mix well.
7) Salt and pepper to taste.

Lemon Green Beans

Total Minutes: 15 Minutes
Prep Time: 10 Minutes
Cook Time: 5 Minutes
Servings: 4

Ingredients

- Olive Oil – 3 Tablespoons
- Butter – 3 Tablespoons
- Fresh Green beans – 1 lb.
- Lemon Pepper
- Salt

Let us get to cooking!

7. In a 9.5" fry pan, heat the olive oil and butter.
8. Add the Green Beans, and lemon pepper.
9. Toss so all the beans are well coated with the oil and butter.
10. Cook until tender.
11. Salt to taste
12. Enjoy.

Yummy Macaroni and Cheese

Total Minutes: 55 Minutes
Prep Time: 10 Minutes
Cook Time: 45 Minutes
Servings: 8

Ingredients

- Macaroni Elbow Pasta – Box 6oz
- Butter - 1 Stick
- Flour - 1 Cup
- Sour Cream - 1 Cup
- Milk - 1 Cup
- Yellow Mustard - ½ Cup
- Fresh Ground Black Pepper – ½ Teaspoon
- Shredded Cheddar Cheese - 2 Cups

Let us get to cooking!

1) Preheat an oven to 350ºF.
2) Cook the Macaroni Elbow Pasta according to the instructions on the box/bag.
3) For the cheese sauce, melt the butter in a 3-quart sauté pan over medium heat.
4) Add flour. Cooked the flour until golden brown. Add sour cream and milk. Continue to stir, cook until smooth. Add mustard and black pepper.
5) Add one bag of cheddar cheese, stir until the cheese has melted
6) Add the cooked macaroni pasta and stir until evenly coated.
7) Pour into a 9" x 9" x 2" Baking Pan. Cover the top with the remaining cheese. Bake 30-35 minutes until Cheese is melted and golden brown on the edges.
8) Enjoy!

Holiday Cornbread Dressing

Total Minutes: 1 Hour 30 Minutes
Prep Time: 30 Minutes
Cook Time: 1 Hour
Servings: 10

Ingredients

- Turkey Necks – 2lbs
- Turkey Wings – 2lbs
- Chicken Liver – 1 Container
- Chicken Gizzards – 1Lbs.
- Onions – 1 Large, Diced
- Bell Peppers – 1, Diced
- Lemon Pepper – 2 Tablespoons
- Onion Powder - 2 Tablespoons
- Garlic Powder - 2 Tablespoons
- Chicken Broth – 3 32oz
- Water as Needed

Let us get to cooking!

1) In a large saucepan add all Ingredients.
2) Pour enough water to cover all the Ingredients. Add more water to keep the ingredients covered as the liquid evaporates while cooking.
3) Cook for 1 hour.
4) Drain the broth in a bowl, Set aside.
5) Let the meat cool. Pull the meat apart from the bones. Cut up the gizzards and livers. Set aside.

Cornbread for Holiday Cornbread Dressing
Ingredients

- Flour - 2 ½ Cups
- Cornmeal - 2 ½ Cups
- Poultry Seasoning - 2 Tablespoons
- Onion – 1 Large, small dice
- Celery – 2 Stalks - Small dice
- Eggs - 2
- Butter – Melted, 2 sticks
- Buttermilk - 3 Cups
- Water - 1 Cups (add more if needed)

Holiday Cornbread Dressing Continued:

Let us get to cooking the cornbread!

1. Preheat oven to 400ºF.
2. Add all the ingredients and half of the melted butter into a large bowl. Mix well.
3. Pour the other half of the melted better into a 9'x13'x2' baking pan.
4. Pour in the mixture.
5. Bake 20-25 minutes.
6. Let cornbread cool, then break into crumbles. Set aside.

Time to assemble

1. Combine all the ingredients (3-4 cups of the broth, meats, and cornbread into a large bowl. Mix well.
2. Pour into a 9" x 9" x 2" Baking Pan. Spread evenly.
3. Bake about 45 minutes or until golden brown. Enjoy

Lemon Pepper or Sweet Potato Chips

Total Minutes: 40 Minutes
Prep Time: 20 Minutes
Cook Time: 20 Minutes
Servings: 4
Ingredients

- Lemon Pepper – 1 Teaspoon
- Red Pepper – 1 Teaspoon
- Salt – ½ Teaspoon
- Russet Potatoes – 2 Large
- Vegetable Oil for deep frying

Sweet Potato Chips

Ingredients

- Cinnamon – 1 Teaspoon
- Allspice – 1 Teaspoon
- Raw Sugar – 2 Tablespoons
- Salt – ½ Teaspoon
- Sweet Potatoes – 2 Large
- Vegetable Oil for deep frying

Let us get to cooking!

1) Peel the potatoes. Using a mandolin (please be extra careful), slice the potatoes on the thin setting or use a knife to slice and cut the potatoes into 1/16-inch slices.
2) Place the sliced potatoes in a bowl of cold water.
3) Fill a 6-quart sauté pan about half-way with vegetable oil, heat to 350ºF.
4) Pat dry the potatoes before frying.
5) Place a handful of the potatoes in the hot oil, cook for 1 minutes. Remove from the oil. The potatoes will be limply. Once you have completed cooking all the sweet potatoes in round one.
6) Return the potatoes to the heated oil a handful at a time, cook an additional 1- 2 minutes. Remove the chips from the oil, place into a strainer to drain the excess oil.
7) Season with the spices. Enjoy!

Dill Potato Salad

Total Minutes: 1 Hour
Prep Time: 30 Minutes
Cook Time: 30 Minutes
Servings: 8

Ingredients

- Russet Potatoes – 6 Peeled, Chopped into bite size pieces
- Water as needed
- Eggs – 3, hard boiled, diced into small pieces
- Dill Pickle Relish – ¾ Cup or chop sliced dill pickles.
- Onion – 1 Finely Chopped
- Bell Pepper – 1 Finely Chopped
- Mustard – ¾ Cup
- Miracle Whip – ¾ Cup

Let us get to cooking

1) In a 3-quart sauté pan boil the potatoes until tender. Drain off the water and set aside to cool.
2) In a large bowl add the remaining ingredients. Mix well.
3) Add the cooked potatoes, coat the potatoes evenly.
4) Pour the potato salad in a serving bowl.
5) Let cool in the refrigerator for 2-3 hours or overnight. Enjoy.

Vinegar Collard Greens with Chicken

Total Minutes: 1 Hour 20 Minutes
Prep Time: 20 Minutes
Cook Time: 1 Hour
Servings: 8

Ingredients

- Chicken Breast – 1 lb.
- Waters 12 Cups
- Lemon Pepper - 2 Tablespoons
- Basil Leaves - 1 Tablespoon
- Crush Rosemary - ½ Tablespoon
- Poultry Seasoning - 1 Tablespoon
- Salt – 1 Teaspoon
- Butter - 6 Tablespoons
- Olive Oil - 3 Tablespoons
- Onion – 1, diced
- Bell Pepper – 1, diced
- Celery – ½ Cup, diced
- White Vinegar – ½ Cup
- Apple Cider Vinegar - ½ /Cup
- Pre-cut Collard Greens – 64 Oz's
- Salt to taste

Let us get to cooking

1) In a 6-quart stockpot, add the chicken breast, water, lemon pepper, basil leaves, crush rosemary, poultry seasoning, butter and 1 teaspoon of salt. Boil for 45 – 1 hour. Pour the broth in a large bowl and the chicken in another bowl to cool. Pull apart the chicken. Set aside.
2) In the same stockpot, heat the olive oil under medium to high heat. Add the onions, bell pepper and celery, cook until tender.
3) Add the white vinegar, apple cider vinegar and 3 cups of the chicken broth. Stir to mix. Add the pulled chicken. Mix well.
4) Fill the pot with some of the greens, once the greens cook down, add more greens, repeat. Cook the greens until tender, salt to taste. Enjoy.

Turmeric Rice with Chicken

Total Minutes: 2 Hours
Prep Time: 30 Minutes
Cook Time: 1 Hour 30 Minutes
Servings: 10

Ingredients

- Vegetable Oil – 3 Tablespoons
- Onion – 1, Chopped
- Bell Peppers – 1 Chopped
- Mince Garlic – 2 Teaspoons
- Water – 9 Cups
- Red Pepper – ½ Teaspoons
- Ground Turmeric – 2 Tablespoons
- Onion Powder – 1 Tablespoon
- Garlic Powder – 1 Tablespoon
- Chicken bouillon – 3 Small
- Chicken Breast – 2, Thigh - 2
- Uncooked White Rice – 4 Cups

Let us get to cooking.

1) Heat the oil in a 6-quart stockpot. Add the onion, bell peppers and minced garlic. Cook until the veggies are tender.
2) Add the water, red pepper, ground turmeric, onion powder, garlic powder, chicken bouillon and chicken. Cook on medium to high heat for 1 hour. Remove from the heat.
3) Carefully, drain the broth into a bowl. Measure 8 Cups of broth and return the broth to the pot. Pull apart the chicken and return to the pot. Heat the broth under medium to high heat. Let the broth come to a boil. Add the rice, reduce heat to medium to low, cook an additional 20-30 minutes.
4) Enjoy!

Creamed Style Corn

Total Minutes: 30 Minutes
Prep Time: 10 Minutes
Cook Time: 20 Minutes
Servings: 4

Ingredients

- Butter – ½ Stick
- Frozen or Fresh Corn – 3-4 ears, kernel cut from cob
- Heavy Cream – 1 Cup
- Salt – ½ Teaspoon
- Freshly Ground Pepper – ½ Teaspoon
- Granulated Sugar – 1 Tablespoon

Let us get to cooking.

1) Melt the butter in a 9.5 fry pan over medium-low heat.
2) Add the heavy cream, salt, pepper, and sugar. Continuously stir until the heavy cream thickens.
3) Add the corn and reduce heat to low. Cook, until heated through.
4) Enjoy.

Fruit Salad with Carrot Sauce

Total Minutes: 20 Minutes
Prep Time: 20 Minutes
Cook Time: 0 Minutes
Servings: 4

Ingredients

- White Grapes (or any of your choice) - 1 Cup, sliced
- Strawberries – 1 Cup, sliced
- Blackberries – 1 Cup
- Cantaloupe – 1 Cup, chopped into cubes
- Honey Dew - 1 Cup, chopped into cubes

Let us get to cooking!

1) Combine all ingredients in a bowl, toss.
2) Serve with the Carrot Sauce below

Carrot Sauce

Ingredients

- Carrots Juice – 1 ½ Cups
- Cream Cheese – 4 oz, Softened
- Vanilla – 1 Teaspoon
- Powdered Sugar – 1 Cup

Let us get to cooking!

1) Combine all ingredients in a blender.
2) Blend until smooth.
3) Enjoy with the fruit salad.

Fried Brown Rice and Onion

Total Minutes: 30 Minutes
Prep Time: 20 Minutes
Cook Time: 10 Minutes
Servings: 4

Ingredients

- Olive Oil, 2 tablespoons and as needed.
- Brown Rice - 4 Cups, Cooked
- Onion – Medium Sized, Sliced
- Salt to taste
- Fresh Ground Pepper to taste

Let us get to cooking!

1) In a 3-quart sauté pan or wok heat oil under medium to high heat.
2) Pour in the onions. Cook until onion corners are golden brown. Stir in cooked rice. Cook until lightly toasted.
3) Salt and pepper to taste. Enjoy.

Cabbage and Brown Rice

Total Minutes: 25 Minutes
Prep Time: 20 Minutes
Cook Time: 15 Minutes
Servings: 4
Ingredients

- Olive Oil, 2 tablespoons and as needed.
- Cabbage – ½ Thinly Sliced
- Cooked Brown Rice – 4 Cups
- Yellow Onion – 1 Medium Sized, Thinly Sliced
- Salt to Taste
- Fresh Ground Pepper to Taste

Let us get to cooking!

1) In a 3-quart sauté pan or wok heat oil under medium to high heat.
2) Pour in the onions. Cook until onion corners are golden brown.
3) Stir in cooked rice. Cook until lightly toasted.
4) Add the cabbage. Cook until tender.
5) Salt and pepper to taste.

Blackened Spicy Okra

Total Minutes: 20 Minutes
Prep Time: 10 Minutes
Cook Time: 10 Minutes
Servings: 4

it is

Ingredients

- Olive Oil – 3- Tablespoons
- Fresh Okra – Diced 4 cups
- 1 Lemon – Shaved lemon peel
- Sweet Peppers – chopped – 2 cups
- Onion – half diced
- Green peppers – half diced
- Red pepper – ¼ teaspoon (caution hot)
- Salt – pinch

Let us get to cooking.

1) Heat the olive oil in a 9.5" fry pan under medium to high heat.
2) Combine all ingredients sauté until blackened on the edges. Enjoy with your favorite chicken or fish.

Creamy Creamed Spinach

Total Minutes: **20 Minutes**
Prep Time: **10 Minutes**
Cook Time: **10 Minutes**
Servings: **4**

Ingredients

- Butter – 2 Tablespoons
- Onion – ¼ Pureed
- Heavy Cream – 1 Cup
- Parmesan Cheese – ½ Cup
- Fresh Spinach – 4 Hands Full

Let us get to cooking.

1) In a 9.5inch fry pan, melt the butter under medium-low heat.
2) Add the pureed onions. Cook until the aroma releases.
3) Add the heavy cream. Cook until the heavy cream thickens. Stir continuously.
4) Add the parmesan cheese, stir as it melts into the creamy sauce.
5) Add the spinach, cook until the spinach withers. Enjoy.

Breads

Southern Cornbread

Total Minutes:	**50 Minutes**
Prep Time:	**20 Minutes**
Cook Time:	**30 Minutes**
Servings:	**10**

Ingredients

- Flour - 2 ½ Cups
- Cornmeal - 2 ½ Cups
- Granulated Sugar – 3 Tablespoons
- Eggs - 2
- Butter - 2 Sticks, melted
- Buttermilk -2 Cups

Let us get to cooking!

1) Preheat oven to 400ºF.
2) Add all the ingredients, but only half of the melted butter into a large bowl. Mix well.
3) Pour other half of the melted better into a 9" x 9" x 2" Baking Pan or 12 count Muffin Pan.
4) Pour in the mixture.
5) Bake 20-25 minutes.
6) Enjoy!

Butter Milk Parmesan Biscuits

Total Minutes:	**40 Minutes**
Prep Time:	**20 Minutes**
Cook Time:	**20 Minutes**
Servings:	**6**

Ingredients

- All Purpose Flour – 3 ½ Cups
- Baking Powder - 2 Teaspoons
- Salt - 1 Teaspoon
- Baking Soda - ¼ Teaspoon
- Cold Butter - 1 ½ Cups (3 sticks), grated or small dice. Tip: Place butter in the freezer overnight.
- Buttermilk – 1 ½ Cups
- Parmesan Cheese – 1 Cup

Let us get to cooking!

1) Preheat oven to 400ºF
2) Line a baking sheet with a silicon mat or ungreased.
3) In a large bowl, sift together flour, baking powder, salt, and baking soda.
4) Add chilled butter to the flour mixture. Gently massage with hands (use gloves or not)
5) Make Well and add buttermilk.
6) Place dough onto a cleaned flour coated surface and lightly knead. Using a rolling pin, lightly roll dough out to ½ inch thickness. Fold dough, lightly roll dough, repeat 3-4 times.
7) Cut dough with a floured biscuit cutter.
8) Place the biscuits about 2 inches apart on the baking sheet.
9) Spread melted butter on top of the biscuits.
10) Bake the biscuits for 10 minutes.
11) Top the biscuits with the parmesan cheese.
12) Bake an additional 5-10, until golden brown.
13) Enjoy.

Banana Walnut and Pecan Bread

Total Minutes: **50 Minutes**
Prep Time: **20 Minutes**
Cook Time: **30 Minutes**
Servings: **10**

Ingredients

- Baking Spray or 2 Tablespoons of Butter
- Self-Rising Flour - 1 ¾ Cups
- Baking Soda – 1 Teaspoon
- Eggs Large - 2, Room Temperature
- Vanilla Extract - ½ Teaspoon
- Unsalted Butter - ½ Cup, Room Temperature
- Sugar – 1 Cup
- Brown Sugar - ½ Cup
- Bananas – 4, Very Ripe, Peeled, Mashed with a Fork (About 1 Cup)
- Walnut Pieces - ½ Cup
- Pecans – ½ Cup
- Miracle Whip - 3 Tablespoons

Let us get to cooking!

1) Preheat the oven to 350ºF.
2) Spray 9" x 5" X 3" Loaf Pan with Pam Baking Spray or use butter to coat the pan.
3) Sift the flour and baking soda, set aside.
4) With an electric mixer, cream the butter and sugars until light and fluffy.
5) Add the eggs and vanilla. Mix.
6) Add the bananas (the mixture will appear frizzy).
7) With a rubber spatula, mix in the flour just to incorporated. Fold in the nuts and transfer the batter to the prepared pan.
8) Bake for 50-55 minutes or until a toothpick inserted into the center of the bread comes out clean.
9) Cool for 5 minutes. Remove from the pan. Enjoy now or the next morning with your favorite cup of coffee.

Cinnamon Pancakes

Total Minutes: **25 Minutes**
Prep Time: **10 Minutes**
Cook Time: **15 Minutes**
Servings: **5**

Ingredients

- Self-Rising Flour – 3 Cups
- Cinnamon – ½ Teaspoon
- Vanilla Extract – 1 Teaspoon
- Granulated Sugar – ½ Cup
- Salt – ¼ Teaspoon
- Butter – 4 Teaspoons, melted
- Milk – 2 ½ Cups

Let us get to cooking.

1) Combine all the ingredients into a mixing bowl. Whisk or use an electric blender to combine all the ingredients into a lump less mixture.
2) Heat a 9.5" fry pan or use an electric griddle, coat with cooking spray. Pour ¼ cup of the batter onto the skillet. Cook until bubbles appear on top. Flip with a spatula and cook until lightly browned on the other side. Enjoy with your favorite syrup or jam.

Blueberry Alexis Muffins

Total Minutes: 3 Hours 20 Minutes
Prep Time: 2 Hours 30 Minutes
Cook Time: 50 Minutes
Servings: 20

Ingredients

- Cake Flour – 2 Cups
- Granulated Sugar – ½ Cup
- Baking Powder – 2 Teaspoons
- Salt - ½ Teaspoon
- Eggs – 1
- Buttermilk – ½ Cup
- Blueberry Juice – ½ Cup
- Vanilla Extract – 1 Teaspoon
- Butter – 4 Tablespoon, Melted
- Blueberries – ½ Cup (Optional)
- Course Cane Sugar

Let us get baking.

1) Line six cups in the muffin pan with cupcake liners.
2) In a mixing bowl add the cake flour, sugar, baking powder and salt. Mix well. Set aside.
3) In another small bowl add the egg, buttermilk, blueberry juice, vanilla extract. Mix well.
4) Add the liquids and melted better to the dry ingredients. Mix well.
5) Gently fold in the blueberries.
6) Evenly pour the batter into six cups in the muffin pan.
7) Sprinkle the top of the batter with the course cane sugar.
8) Bake for 20 minutes. Enjoy!

Cinnamon Dough Rolls

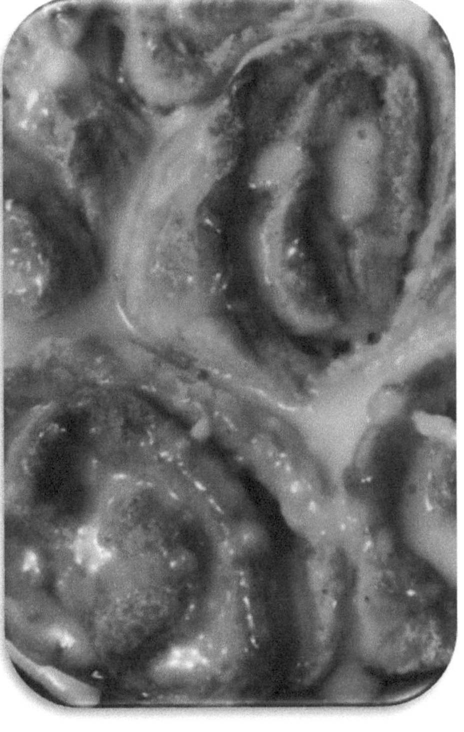

Total Minutes: 3 Hours 20 Minutes
Prep Time: 2 Hours 30 Minutes
Cook Time: 50 Minutes
Servings: 10

Ingredients

- Sweet Potatoes – 1 Coarsely Chopped
  Mashed Sweet Potatoes – ½ Cup
- Water from the boiled Sweet Potatoes – ½ Cup
- Butter – ½ Cup
- Sugar – ½ Cup
- Salt – 1 Teaspoons
- Hot Water – ½ Cup
- Instant Dry Yeast, 1 pack
- Eggs – 1
- All Purpose Flour – 4 Cups

Let us get to cooking!

1) In a 2.5quart saucepan, boil the chopped sweet potatoes until tender. Remove the potatoes and reserve ½ cup of the sweet potato water.
2) In a large bowl combine the ½ cup of the mashed sweet potatoes, reserved sweet potato water, butter, sugar, salt, hot water, set aside.
3) In another large bowl combine the Instant Dry Yeast and all-purpose flour, stir together. Set aside.
4) Add the egg to the potato mixture, stir, then add flour mixture- two cups at a time. Knead 5 to 7 minutes
5) Place the dough in a bowl greased with olive oil, coat the dough with the olive oil, then cover with a dish towel to rise about 1 hour in a warm spot. The dough should double in size.
6) In the meantime, make the cinnamon filling and icing.

Cinnamon Filling Ingredients

- Butter - 1 Stick Softened
- Brown Sugar – 1 Cup
- Cinnamon – 2 Tablespoons

Cinnamon Dough Rolls Continued:

Let us get to cooking

1) Combine all ingredients, mix well. Set aside.

Icing Ingredients

- Powdered Sugar – 3 ½ Cups
- Cream Cheese – 1 8 Ounce Block, Softened
- Milk or Water – 6-8 Tablespoons or More If Needed

Let us get to cooking.

1) Combine all Ingredients, mix well

Time to assemble.

2) Remove the dough from the bowl, punch the dough with your fist, cut dough in half
3) Roll the dough into a rectangle onto a surface lightly coated with flour. Spread the cinnamon mixture on the dough evenly. Roll the dough lengthwise. Place in the refrigerator for 30 minutes. Preheat oven to 350ºF.
4) Cut the dough into 10 slices. Place on greased cookie sheet or hotel pan.
5) Bake for 25 to 30 minutes. Pour the icing over the hot rolls. Enjoy!

Desserts

Pretty Peachy Pie

Total Minutes: 1 Hour 20 Minutes
Prep Time: 30 Minutes
Cook Time: 50 Minutes
Servings: 8

Ingredients for Crust

- All Purpose Flour 2 ½ Cups
- Salt 1 teaspoon
- Cold Butter - 1 ½ Sticks, grated
- Cold Water ¼ Cup
- Egg – 1 (for Egg Wash)

Let us make the Crust.

1) In a large bowl, sift together flour and salt.
2) Add chilled butter to the flour mixture. Gently massage with your hands.
3) Add cold water. Add more if the dough is dry.
4) Place dough onto a cleaned floured surface and lightly knead for 5 minutes.
5) Roll the dough in a ball, wrap with plastic wrap or place in a plastic bag. Chill for 1 hour. In the meantime, make the filling.

Ingredients for the Peach Filling

- Granulated Sugar - 2 Cups
- Allspice – 1 Teaspoon
- Nutmeg - ½ Teaspoon
- Ground Cinnamon - 1 Teaspoon
- Cornstarch – ½ Cup
- Fresh Peaches – Peeled and cut into slices.
- Tip: Freeze the peaches, let defrost, pull the skin away
- Lemon Juice - ¼ Cup
- Butter - ½ Cup
- Water – ¾ Cup

Let us make the Peach Filling.

1) In a bowl, mix the sugar, allspice, nutmeg, ground cinnamon, and cornstarch. Set aside.
2) In a 3-quart sauté pan, heat the peaches, lemon juice, water, and butter under medium to low heat until it comes to a simmer. Add the dry ingredients. Cook until filling thickens. Remove from heat and set aside.

Time to assemble

1) Pre-heat the oven to 350ºF.
2) Cut dough in half. Using a rolling pin, lightly roll dough out to ¼ inch thickness. Make sure the dough will cover the 9" x 9" x 2" pie pan. Repeat for the top layer.
3) Place the dough in the pie pan, press against the side of the pan. Roll the dough that is overlapping the pie pan up against the top of the pan. Add the filling.
4) Place the top layer of dough, again, roll the dough that is overlapping the pie pan against the top of the pan. Pinch the two layers of dough together. Cut slices into the top layer for venting.
5) Crack the egg into a small bowl add 1 tablespoon of water. Mix well for the egg wash. Using a basting brush, coat the top of the pie crust with the egg wash to make the crush shine.
6) Bake for 45 minutes to an hour. Enjoy.

Brown Sugar, Sugar Cookies

Total Minutes: 22-24 Minutes
Prep Time: 15 Minutes
Cook Time: 7-9 Minutes
Servings: 6

Ingredients

- All Purpose Flour 2 cups
- Baking Soda - 1/2 Teaspoon
- Baking Powder - 1/2 Teaspoon
- Salt – 1 Teaspoon
- Unsalted Butter - 1 cup (2 sticks), room temperature
- Light Brown Sugar – 2 Cups
- Eggs - 2
- vanilla extract –2 Teaspoons
- Granulated Sugar – ½ Cup

Let us get to cooking!

1) Preheat oven to 350ºF.
2) Line baking sheets with silicone baking mats or parchment paper.
3) In a large bowl combine the flour, baking soda, baking powder and salt, set aside.
4) In a large mixing bowl cream together butter and brown sugar with a hand mixer.
5) Add the eggs, mix well. Add the vanilla. Mix well.
6) Fold in the flour mixture, mix until the dry ingredients are combined.
7) Place dough in the refrigerator for 1 hour.
8) Using a tablespoon, spoon the cookie dough and roll into a ball. Roll the cookie dough ball in the granulated sugar. Place the cookie dough on the cookie sheet, press down.
9) Bake 9-10 minutes. Let Cool. Enjoy.

Southern Apple Pie

Total Minutes: 1 Hour 10 Minutes
Prep Time: 20 Minutes
Cook Time: 50 Minutes
Servings:

Ingredients for the Crust

- All Purpose Flour 2 ½ Cups
- Salt 1 teaspoon
- Cold Butter - 1 ½ Sticks, grated
- Cold Water ¼ Cup
- Egg – 1 (for Egg Wash)

Let us get prepping the Crust

1) In a large bowl, sift together flour and salt.
2) Add chilled butter to the flour mixture. Gently massage with your hands.
3) Add cold water. Add more if the dough is dry.
4) Place dough onto a cleaned floured surface and lightly knead for 5 minutes.
5) Roll the dough in a ball, wrap with plastic wrap or place in a plastic bag. Chill for 1 hour.
6) In the meantime, make the filling.

Filling Ingredients

- Apples – 6-7, peeled and sliced
- Water – 1 ¼ Cup
- Sugar 1 ½ Cups
- Flour - 3 TBSP
- Salt - ½ teaspoon
- Cinnamon - 1 teaspoon
- Nutmeg - ¼ teaspoons
- Lemon - ½, squeezed or 2 tablespoons of lemon juice from concentrate.
- Cornstarch – ¼ Cup

Let us get to cooking the apple filling

1) In a 3-quart sauté pan add the apples, water (1cup), sugar, flour, salt, cinnamon, nutmeg, and lemon juice. Cook under medium heat until apples are tender. Stirring occasionally. Combine the remaining water with the cornstarch, stir well. Pour in the apple filling to thicken. Continuously stir to prevent the filling from sticking to the bottom of the pan. Remove from heat, set aside.

Time to assemble

1) Pre-heat the oven to 350ºF.
2) Cut dough in half. Using a rolling pin, lightly roll dough out to ¼ inch thickness. Make sure the dough will cover the 9" x 9" x 2" pie pan. Repeat for the top layer.
3) Place the dough in the pie pan, press against the side of the pan. Cut the excess dough to the size of the pie pan.
4) Add the filling.
5) Place the top layer of dough, again, cut the excess dough that is overlapping to the size of the pie pan. Pinch the two layers of dough together. Cut slices into the top layer for venting
6) Crack the egg into a small bowl add 1 tablespoon of water. Mix well for the egg wash. Using a basting brush, coat the top of the pie crust with the egg wash to make the crush shine.
7) Bake for 45 minutes to an hour. Enjoy.

Bundt Me Carrot Cake

Total Minutes: 1 Hour 10 Minutes
Prep Time: 40 Minutes
Cook Time: 30 Minutes
Servings: 8

Ingredients for the Carrot Cake

- Brown Sugar – 2 Cups
- Vegetable Oil -1 Cup
- Eggs - 4
- All-Purpose Flour – 3 Cups
- Baking Soda – 2 Teaspoons
- Salt – 1 Teaspoon
- Ground Cinnamon – 2 Teaspoons
- Nutmeg – 1 Teaspoon
- Ground Cloves – ¼ Teaspoon
- Raw Finely Ground Carrots – 5 Cups
- Mayonnaise – 3 Tablespoons
- Pecan – 1 Cup, Chopped

Cream Cheese Sauce Ingredients

- Cream Cheese – 1 8oz Block – room temperature
- Carrot Juice – ½ Cup
- Powdered Sugar – 2 Cups
- Lemon Juice – ½ Cup
- For a looser icing add more carrot juice.

Let us get to cooking!

1) Preheat oven to 300ºF.
2) Grease a 10” Bundt Pan. Set aside.
3) In a mixing bowl, mix sugar, vegetable oil, and eggs
4) In another bowl, sift together flour, baking soda, salt, and cinnamon
5) Fold dry ingredients into wet mixture and blend well.
6) Fold in carrots
7) Add the Mayonnaise, mix well
8) Fold in the pecans until well blended.

9) Pour batter into Bundt pan. Bake for 1 hour. Check for doneness by sticking a toothpick in the cake. If the toothpick come out clean, remove from the oven. Let cool.
10) In the meantime, make the frosting.

Let us make the Cream Cheese Frosting

1) Place all the ingredients in a blender. Blend until smooth.
2) Pour over the cake. Enjoy!

Chocolate Pecan & Walnut Peanut Butter Nugget

Total Minutes: 30 Minutes
Prep Time: 20 Minutes
Cook Time: 10 Minutes
Servings: 8

Ingredients

- Milk Chocolate Chips, 11.5 Oz. Bag
- Creamy Peanut Butter - ¾ Cup
- Pecans – 1 Cup, Chopped
- Walnuts – 1 Cup, Chopped

Let us get to cooking.

1) Place cupcake liners in a muffin pan. Set aside.
2) Place the peanut butter in a small glass bowl. Melt in the microwave for 30 – 45 seconds.
3) Pour the chocolate chips in a medium sized glass bowl. Place the bowl in the microwave. Melt the chocolate in 1-minute increments. After each minute stir the chocolate. Repeat until the chocolate has melted.
4) Pour a small amount of the chocolate into the cupcake liners. Add the melted peanut butter. Evenly place the pecan and walnuts in each cupcake liner. Pour additional chocolate on top of the nuts. Top off with each additional nut. Let cool in the refrigerator to solidify. Enjoy.

My Favourite Cream Cheese Cake

Total Minutes: 1 Hour 35 Minutes
Prep Time: 20 Minutes
Cook Time: 1 hour 15 Minutes
Servings: 12

Ingredients

- Cream Cheese – 3 8oz Blocks, Room Temperature.
- Butter - 1 1/2 Cups, Room Temperature
- Granulated Sugar - 3 Cups
- Eggs - 6, Room Temperature
- Vanilla Extract - 1 Teaspoon
- Cake Flour – 3 ½ Cups

Let us get to cooking!

1) Pre-heat the oven to 320ºF.
2) Grease a 10" Bundt cake pan with butter and flour or use a baking spray.
3) Sift the flour in a medium sized bowl. Set aside.
4) In a mixing bowl, cream the butter and 1 ½ 8oz Blocks (12oz) of cream cheese with an electric mixer until smooth.
5) Add the sugar, beat until fluffy. Add vanilla. Mix.
6) Add the eggs two at a time, beating well.
7) Gradually add the flour. Make sure the wipe down the sides of the bowl to incorporate all the ingredients.
8) Pour the batter into the 10-inch Bundt pan. Bake at 320ºF for 1 hour and 15 minutes.
9) Check doneness by sticking a toothpick into the middle of the cake. If the toothpick is clean, remove from the oven. Let cool 5 minutes before flipping the cake out of the cake pan on to a serving plate. Enjoy.

Buttermilk Cream Cheese Icing

Ingredients

- Cream Cheese – 1 ½ 8oz Blocks (12oz) Room Temperature
- Powdered Sugar – 2 Cups
- Butter Milk – ¾ Cup
- Vanilla – 1 Teaspoon

Let us get to cooking.

1) Place all the ingredients in a blender. Blend until smooth and fluffy. Enjoy!
2) Pour the icing over the cake. Enjoy!

Delicious Banana Pudding

Total Minutes: 1 Hour 5 Minutes
Prep Time: 30 Minutes
Cook Time: 15- 20 Minutes
Servings: 5

Ingredients

- Granulated Sugar -1 Cups
- All-Purpose Flour – ½ Cup
- Eggs – 3, Beaten
- Heavy Cream – 2 ½ Cups
- Vanilla Extract – 1 ½ Teaspoons
- Unsalted Butter - 5 Tablespoons, Softened
- Cream Cheese – 1 8oz Block, Softened
- Milk – 2 Cups
- Bananas 3-4
- Vanilla Wafers - (15oz Box)

Let us get to cooking!

1. In 3-quart saucepan, combine the sugar and flour. Mix before turning on the heat.
2. Add the eggs and heavy cream. Stir well.
3. Cook over medium to low heat for 10 – 15 minutes or until thickened.
4. When mixture begins to thicken, remove from heat.
5. Pour batter into a mixing bowl.
6. Add the butter, cream cheese, vanilla, and milk. Blend with a mixture. Set aside.
7. Layer Cookies at the bottom of a medium sized bowl.
8. Slice a banana, layer over the cookies.
9. Pour the filling on top.
10. Add another layer of cookies and bananas.
11. Chill at least one hour in refrigerator before serving.

No Crust Cheesecake

Total Minutes: 1 Hour 35 Minutes
Prep Time: 35 Minutes
Cook Time: 1 Hour
Servings: 8-10

Ingredients

- Granulated Sugar -2 ½ Cups
- All-Purpose Flour - 1 Cup
- Eggs – 3, Beaten
- Heavy Cream - 5 Cups
- Vanilla Extract – 1 ½ Teaspoons
- Unsalted Butter - 5 Tablespoons, Softened
- Lemon Zest – 2 Tablespoons
- Lemon Juice - 3 Tablespoons
- Cream Cheese – 4 8oz Block, Softened
- Milk – 1 Cups

Let us get to cooking!

1. Wrap a 9" x 3" Springform Pan with heavy duty foil to prevent spillage. Set aside
2. In 3-quart saucepan combine: sugar, flour eggs and continuously stir well.
3. Stir in the heavy cream, and cook over low heat, stirring constantly.
4. Cook under low to medium heat for 10 minutes – 15 minutes or until thickened.
5. When mixture begins to thicken, remove from heat.
6. Pour batter into a mixing bowl.
7. Add the butter, cream cheese, vanilla, and milk. Mix with a blender.
8. Pour hot water in a small oven safe pan. Place on the bottom rack of the oven.
9. Pour the batter into the springform pan. Bake on the top rack.
10. Bake for 1 hour. The batter will be loose.
11. Chill overnight in refrigerator.
12. Enjoy as is or top with your favorite fruit topping.

Topping Ingredients

- Frozen or Fresh Strawberries – 2 pints, washed, remove the greenery.
- Strawberry Jam

Let us get to cooking the topping

- Place the strawberries on top of the cheesecake.
- Melt the strawberry jam in a 1.5-quart pan.
- Spoon the hot jam over the strawberries and cheesecake.
- Let cool. Enjoy!

Chewy Coconut & Pecan Cookies

Total Minutes: 22-24 Minutes
Prep Time: 15 Minutes
Cook Time: 7-9 Minutes
Servings: 6

Ingredients

- All-Purpose Flour - 1 ¼ Cup
- Wheat Pastry Flour - 1 ¼ Cup
- Almond Flour - ½ Cup
- Baking Soda - ½ Teaspoon
- Salt - 1 Teaspoon
- Butter – 2 Sticks, Room Temperature
- Brown Sugar - 1 Cup
- Granulated Sugar - ½ Cup
- Eggs - 2
- Vanilla - 2 Teaspoons
- Sweet Coconut Flakes - 1 Cup
- Chopped Pecans - 1 Cup

Let us get to cooking!

1) Preheat oven to 350ºF.
2) Line baking sheets with silicone baking mats or parchment paper.
3) In a large bowl combine the flours, baking soda, baking powder and salt, set aside.
4) In a large mixing bowl cream together butter, brown sugar, and granulated sugar with a hand mixer.
5) Add the eggs, mix well. Add the vanilla. Mix well.
6) Add the flour mixture, mix until the dry ingredients are combined.
7) Fold in the sweet coconut flakes and pecans. Place dough in the refrigerator for 1 hour.
8) Using a tablespoon, spoon the cookie dough and roll into a ball.
9) Place the cookie dough on the cookie sheet about 2 inches apart, press down. Bake 8-10 minutes. Let Cool. Enjoy.

Almond Peanut Butter Cookies

Total Minutes: 22-24 Minutes
Prep Time: 15 Minutes
Cook Time: 7-9 Minutes
Servings: 6

Ingredients

- All-Purpose Flour – 1 ½ Cup
- Almond Flour – 1 ½ Cup
- Salt – 1 Teaspoon
- Baking Powder – 1 Teaspoon
- Baking Soda – 1 Teaspoon
- Unsalted Butter - 2 sticks, room temperature
- Dark Brown Sugar – 1 Cup
- Granulated Sugar – 1 Cup
- Vanilla – 1 Teaspoon
- Eggs – 2
- Creamy Peanut Butter – 1 Cup
- Almonds – ½ Cup

Let us get to cooking!

1) Preheat oven to 350ºF.
2) Line baking sheets with silicone baking mats or parchment paper.
3) In a large bowl combine the flours, baking soda, baking powder and salt, set aside.
4) In a large mixing bowl cream together butter, dark brown sugar, and granulated sugar with a hand mixer. Add the eggs, mix well. Add the vanilla. Mix in the creamy peanut butter. Add the flour mixture, mix until the dry ingredients are combined.
5) Fold in the almonds. Place dough in the refrigerator for 1 hour.
6) Using a tablespoon, spoon the cookie dough and roll into a ball.
7) Place the cookie dough on the cookie sheet, press down.
8) Bake 9-10 minutes. Let Cool. Enjoy.

Double Chocolate Cookies

Total Minutes: 22-24 Minutes
Prep Time: 15 Minutes
Cook Time: 7-9 Minutes
Servings: 6

Ingredients

- Flour - 2 Cups
- Coco Powder - 3/4 Cups
- Salt - 1/8 Teaspoon
- Baking Soda - 1 Teaspoon
- Butter - 2 Sticks
- Granulated Sugar - 2 Cups
- Eggs - 2
- Vanilla – 1 Teaspoon
- Semi-Sweet Chocolate Morsels – 1 Cup

Let us get to cooking!

1) Preheat oven to 350ºF.
2) Line baking sheets with silicone baking mats or parchment paper.
3) In a large bowl combine the flour, baking soda, coco powder and salt, set aside.
4) In a large mixing bowl cream together butter, brown sugar, and granulated sugar with a hand mixer. Add the eggs, mix well. Add the vanilla. Add the flour mixture, mix until the dry ingredients are combined.
5) Add the semi-sweet chocolate morsels.
6) Place dough in the refrigerator for 1 hour.
7) Using a tablespoon, spoon the cookie dough and roll into a ball.
8) Place the cookie dough on the cookie sheet about 2 inches apart, press down.
9) Bake 9-10 minutes. Let Cool. Enjoy

Warm Me Up Drinks

Hazelnut Mocha

Total Minutes: 10 Minutes
Prep Time: 7 Minutes
Cook Time: 3 Minutes
Servings: 1

Ingredients

- Instant Coffee - 2 Teaspoons
- Hazelnut Creamer - ¼ Cup
- Unsweetened Cocoa Powder -1 Teaspoon
- Granulated Sugar -2 Tablespoons
- Whipped Cream

Let us get warm

1) Heat water in a teakettle or a 1.5-quart saucepan. Bring water to a boil.
2) Add the instant coffee, hazelnut creamer, unsweetened cocoa powder, and sugar to a 16oz coffee cup.
3) Add the hot water. Stir to mix all the ingredients.
4) Top with whipped cream.
5) Enjoy!

Ingredients for Whipped Cream

- Heavy Cream – ½ Cup
- Granulated Sugar – 2 Teaspoons

Let us get blending

1) Pour the heavy cream into a personal blender. Blend 30 -45 seconds. Heavy cream should be thick.
2) Add the sugar, blend another 10 seconds. Add to the top of your beverage. Enjoy!

Mint Raspberry Tea

Total Minutes: 17 Minutes
Prep Time: 7 Minutes
Cook Time: 10 Minutes
Servings: 1

Ingredients

- Water – 2 Cups
- Fresh Raspberries – 1 Cup, mashed
- Mint Leaves – 3-4
- Lime Juice – 1 Teaspoon
- Granulated Sugar -2 Tablespoons

Let us get warm.

1) Heat the water in a 1.5-quart saucepan. Bring water to a boil.
2) Add the raspberries. Let boil for 3 - 5 minutes.
3) Place cheesecloth in a small bowl. Enough to overlay the sides of the bowl.
4) Pour the raspberries, mint leaves, and raspberry tea in the cheesecloth to catch the blackberries remnants. Discard the remnants.
5) Pour the cranberry tea in a 16oz teacup.
6) Add the sugar. Stir to combine.
7) Enjoy.

Peppermint Chocolate

Total Minutes: 10 Minutes
Prep Time: 7 Minutes
Cook Time: 3 Minutes
Servings: 1

Ingredients

- Milk – 2 Cups
- Unsweetened Cocoa Powder -1 Teaspoon
- Granulated Sugar -2 Tablespoons
- Peppermint Oil – 1 drop
- Whipped Cream

Let us get warm.

1) Heat the milk in a 1.5-quart saucepan.
2) Add the unsweetened cocoa powder and sugar to a 16oz coffee cup.
3) Add the hot milk. Stir to mix all the ingredients.
4) Add the peppermint oil, stir.
5) Top with whipped cream.
6) Enjoy

Ingredients for Whipped Cream

- Heavy Cream – ½ Cup
- Granulated Sugar – 2 Teaspoons

Let us get blending

1) Pour the heavy cream into a personal blender. Blend 30 -45 seconds. Heavy cream should be thick.
2) Add the sugar, blend another 10 seconds. Add to the top of your beverage. Enjoy
3) Enjoy!

Cranberry Tea

Total Minutes: 17 Minutes
Prep Time: 7 Minutes
Cook Time: 10 Minutes
Servings: 1

Ingredients

- Water – 2 Cups
- Fresh Cranberries – 1 Cup, Mashed
- Lime Juice – 1 Teaspoon
- Granulated Sugar -2 Tablespoons

Let us get warm

1) Heat the water in a 1.5-quart saucepan. Bring water to a boil.
2) Add the cranberries. Let boil for 3 – 5 minutes. Be careful, the cranberries will pop when they get hot.
3) Place cheesecloth in a small bowl. Enough to overlay the sides of the bowl.
4) Pour the cranberries and cranberry tea in the cheesecloth to catch the blackberries remnants. Discard the remnants.
5) Pour the cranberry tea in a 16oz teacup.
6) Add the lime juice and sugar. Stir to combine.
7) Enjoy.

Spicy Vanilla Coffee

Total Minutes: 10 Minutes
Prep Time: 7 Minutes
Cook Time: 3 Minutes
Servings: 1

Ingredients

1. Instant Coffee - 2 Teaspoons
2. Vanilla Creamer – ¼ Cup
3. Allspice - ¼ Teaspoon
4. Red Pepper – Sprinkle
5. Granulated Sugar -2 Tablespoons
6. Whipped Cream

Let us get warm

1) Heat water in a teakettle or a 1.5-quart saucepan. Bring water to a boil.
2) Add the instant coffee, vanilla creamer, allspice, red pepper, and sugar to a 16oz coffee cup.
3) Add the hot water. Stir to mix all the ingredients.
4) Top with whipped cream.
5) Enjoy!

Ingredients for Whipped Cream

- Heavy Cream – ½ Cup
- Granulated Sugar – 2 Teaspoons

Let us get blending

1) Pour the heavy cream into a personal blender. Blend 30 -45 seconds. Heavy cream should be thick.
2) Add the sugar, blend another 10 seconds. Add to the top of your beverage. Enjoy
3) Enjoy!

Black Berry Tea

Total Minutes: 12 Minutes
Prep Time: 7 Minutes
Cook Time: 5 Minutes
Servings: 1

Ingredients

- Water – 2 Cups
- Blackberries – ½ Cup, mashed
- Lemon Juice – 1 Teaspoon
- Granulated Sugar -2 Tablespoons

Let us get warm

1) Heat the water in a 1.5-quart saucepan. Bring water to a boil.
2) Add the blackberries. Let boil for 3 minutes.
3) Place cheesecloth in a small bowl. Enough to overlay the sides of the bowl.
4) Pour the blackberries in the cheesecloth to catch the blackberries remnants. Discard the remnants.
5) Pour the blackberry tea in a 16oz teacup.
6) Add the lemon juice and sugar. Stir to combine.
7) Enjoy.

Winter in Florida Drinks

Lime Sweet Tea

Total Minutes: **5 Minutes**
Prep Time: **3 Minutes**
Cook Time: **0 Minutes**
Servings: **1**

Ingredients

- Ready Made Sweet Tea - 1 Cup
- Limeade - 1-2 Teaspoons
- Ice as needed

Let us get drinking!

1) Pour the ready-made sweet tea into a tall glass.
2) Add the lime juice. Stir well.
3) Add the ice. Enjoy!

Mixed Berry Slushy

Total Minutes: **5 Minutes**
Prep Time: **3 Minutes**
Cook Time: **0 Minutes**
Servings: **1**

Ingredients

- Blackberries – ½ Cup
- Raspberries - ½ Cup
- Strawberries – ½ Cup
- Blueberries – ½ Cup
- Sugar to taste (substitute with Honey or Agave)

Let us get drinking.

1) Add all ingredients in a hand blender. Blend until the fruits are crushed.
2) Add the sugar to taste. Blend well. Enjoy!

Kiwi Pear Slushy

Total Minutes: 5 Minutes
Prep Time: 3 Minutes
Cook Time: 0 Minutes
Servings: 1

Ingredients

- Frozen Pear – 1 Cup
- Frozen Kiwi – 1 Cup
- Sugar to taste (substitute with Honey or Agave)

Let us get drinking.

1) Add all ingredients in a hand blender. Blend until the fruits are crushed.
2) Add the sugar to taste. Blend well. Enjoy!

Blackberry Cantaloupe

Total Minutes: 5 Minutes
Prep Time: 3 Minutes
Cook Time: 0 Minutes
Servings: 1

Ingredients

- Frozen Blackberries – 1 Cups
- Frozen Cantaloupe – 1 Cup
- Sugar to taste (substitute with Honey or Agave)

Let us get drinking.

1) Add all ingredients in a hand blender. Blend until the fruits are crushed.
2) Add the sugar to taste. Blend well. Enjoy!

Pomegranate Blueberry

Total Minutes: 5 Minutes
Prep Time: 3 Minutes
Cook Time: 0 Minutes
Servings: 1

Ingredients

- Frozen Pomegranate Juice – 1 Cup
- Frozen Strawberries - 1 Cups
- Sugar to taste (substitute with Honey or Agave)
- Blueberries – ¼ Cup

Let us get drinking.

1) Add all ingredients in a hand blender. Blend until the fruits are crushed.
2) Add the sugar to taste. Blend well.
3) Garnish with the blueberries. Enjoy!

Mango, Carrot and Cantaloupe

Total Minutes: 5 Minutes
Prep Time: 3 Minutes
Cook Time: 0 Minutes
Servings: 1

Ingredients

- Frozen Mango – ½ Cup
- Frozen Carrots – ½ Cup
- Frozen Cantaloupe – ½ Cup
- Seltzer water - ½ Cup
- Sugar to taste (substitute with Honey or Agave)

Let us get drinking.

1) Add all ingredients in a hand blender. Blend until the fruits are crushed.
2) Add the sugar to taste. Blend well. Enjoy!

Honeydew

Total Minutes:	**5 Minutes**
Prep Time:	**3 Minutes**
Cook Time:	**0 Minutes**
Servings:	**1**

Ingredients

- Frozen Honeydew – 1 Cup
- Sugar to taste (substitute with Honey or Agave)

Let us get drinking.

1) Add all ingredients in a hand blender. Blend until the fruits are crushed.
2) Add the sugar to taste. Blend well. Enjoy!

Blackberry Kiwi

Total Minutes:	**5 Minutes**
Prep Time:	**3 Minutes**
Cook Time:	**0 Minutes**
Servings:	**1**

Ingredients

- Frozen Blackberries – 1 Cup
- Frozen Kiwi – 1 Cup
- Sugar to taste (substitute with Honey or Agave)

Let us get drinking.

1) Add all ingredients in a hand blender. Blend until the fruits are crushed.
2) Add the sugar to taste. Blend well. Enjoy!

Watermelon Lime

Total Minutes: 5 Minutes
Prep Time: 3 Minutes
Cook Time: 0 Minutes
Servings: 1

Ingredients

- Frozen Watermelon – 1 Cup
- Lime Juice – 2 Teaspoons
- Sugar to taste (substitute with Honey or Agave)

Let us get drinking.

1) Add all ingredients in a hand blender. Blend until the fruits are crushed.
2) Add the sugar to taste. Blend well. Enjoy!

Sugar Kiss Slushy

Total Minutes: 5 Minutes
Prep Time: 3 Minutes
Cook Time: 0 Minutes
Servings: 1

Ingredients

- Frozen Sugar Kiss Melon – 1 Cup
- Sugar to taste (substitute with Honey or Agave)

Let us get drinking.

1) Add all ingredients in a hand blender. Blend until the fruits are crushed.
2) Add the sugar to taste. Blend well. Enjoy!

Copeland's Culinary Eats

Eat and Drink Responsibly!

Index

Thanks to my family for your input, advice and contribution to help make my first cookbook a success. Much Love!

Printed in the USA
CPSIA information can be obtained
at www.ICGtesting.com
LVHW060857080124
768330LV00036B/38

* 9 7 8 0 5 7 8 7 9 6 6 2 8 *